CERAMICS Handbook

N. Richard Hyman

219 Park Avenue South, New York, N.Y. 10003

Contents

Clay Work as a Hobby 4
  Tools and Devices 5
  How to Make a Wedging Board . . 6
  Types of Clay 7
  How to Make a Plaster Bat 9
  Slip 10
  Things You Can Easily Make with Clay 11

Forming an Object with Clay 12
  Designs and Shapes 14
  Construction Methods 16

Sculpting 20
  How to Use Grog 22
  Molding Figurines 24

Molds and Mold Making 26
  The One-piece Mold 28
  The Two-piece Mold 31

Slip Casting 34

Fettling 38

Decorating Your Ceramic Ware 42
  How to Make Engobe 44

Kilns and How to Construct Them . . . 48
  Representative Refractory Shapes . . 55

Preparing for Bisque Firing 60

Operating the Kiln 64

Temperature Equivalents of
  Pyrometric Cones 66
  Devices and Instruments 67
  Operation of a Kiln for Bisque Firing 70

Glazes and How to Apply Them . . . 74
  How to Prepare a Glaze 76

  Recipes for Low Temperature Glazes 78
  Glaze Application 80
  Glost or Glaze Firing 82
  Underglaze 84
  Common Glazing Faults 85

Tiles and Dinnerware 86

Jewelry and Lacework 90

Build a Potter's Wheel 94
  How to Make a Whirler 95
  How to Construct a Kickwheel . . . 96
  The Power Wheel 97

Using the Potter's Wheel 98
  Repairs to Pottery 99
  The Modern Potter's Wheel and its
    Accessories 100
  Throwing on a Potter's Wheel . . . 102

How to Throw a Curved Pitcher . . 104

You Can Make Your Hobby Pay 106

Glossary of Ceramic Terms 111

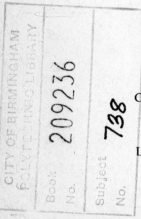

Fourth Printing, 1977

Published by Arco Publishing Company, Inc.
219 Park Avenue South, New York, N.Y. 10003
by arrangement with Fawcett Publications, Inc.

Library of Congress Catalog Card Number 59-13674
ISBN 0-668-00347-2 (Library Edition)
ISBN 0-668-04066-1 (Paper Edition)

Printed in the United States of America

Introduction

Author N. Richard Hyman

CERAMICS is the art of modeling, shaping, or otherwise forming plastic material (clay) into finished objects, usually treated by heat to create a permanence in the otherwise plastic material. This art has developed commercially to become one of the most stable in the world, one upon which rests a large portion of the economy of several nations. In addition, there is an ever-increasing group of hobbyists whose activities are encouraged by the extensive educational programs conducted by practically all public and private institutions throughout the United States. These facilities are not limited to the young students, but are also open to the public at large. Many of these institutions are supported by state subsidy, thereby still further reducing the cost of equipment, material, and instruction. Many of these instructional centers concentrate on various types of specialties in the ceramics field.

By far the most popular courses are those that treat ceramics as a fine art. Here the student learns the basic handling of ceramic material and the various applications and practices which render a lump of clay into a thing of beauty and utility. Only the potter knows the thrill of seeing his first piece come out of the kiln.

Many readers of this book will have had no previous experience with the procedures used in ceramics. For the benefit of these readers, the author here describes briefly the method of making a typical piece of ware, step-by-step from the original clay to the finished piece. You will find, as you explore the chapters in this book which elaborate on these steps, that the basic process in forming any piece is standard, with only variations in the basic materials or equipment used in creating your pieces.

Here is a brief outline of the six basic steps you will take in forming your pieces of ware:

1. Wedging the clay.
2. Forming the object from clay.
3. Fettling (cleaning) the piece.
4. Bisque firing.
5. Glazing the bisque-fired piece.
6. Glost or glaze firing.

3

Clay Work as a Hobby

**One of the oldest of the arts, claycraft is also one of the
most satisfying. The tools are simple and the work is fun.**

TO BEGIN clay work as a hobby, it is necessary to obtain simple materials and tools. You will require a small amount of clay, possibly five pounds, which may be obtained in small quantities from a retail dealer; a table or other working surface covered with a piece of oilcloth wrong side up; an inexpensive rolling pin which may be purchased either in a toy shop or at your local chain store; a box of toothpicks; a paper pie plate; a small amount of building plaster; an orange stick and a clothespin (or another piece of seasoned wood which can be whittled); a small piece of soapless steel wool (a grade used in your home); a sheet of grade 00 sandpaper; a paring knife and either a scrape or a spatula; a coarse sponge, and a small facial sponge. All of these materials can be purchased at your hardware store, except for the clay.

The next step is to determine your location of work. This may be any place, except directly under the eaves of a building or in direct exposure to extreme heat or extreme dampness. There should be fairly good light for working, and there should be either running water or water accessible.

Ceramic Terms

A glossary of terms used in ceramic work will be found in an alphabetical listing beginning on page 111.

4

Tools and Devices

Many other materials and supplies are useful for starting a clay hobby work shop. There are for example, boxwood tools available through hobby shops if you do not care to make them. An ordinary tea strainer is helpful, but this can be readily substituted by nailing together four pieces of wood, secured together to form a square or a rectangle, without top or bottom, and a piece of window screen nailed across the bottom.

Several inexpensive paint brushes are necessary. The writer would suggest a number 3—5—7 water-color brush and at least one ¼" and one ¾" flat tipped brush.

A pitcher or two, preferably of enameled metal or of crockery, are to be desired. In the event that pitchers are not available, large tin cans with a lacquered inner surface, such as the cans used for preserved fruit, may be readily substituted. A spout may be formed by pinching a portion of the rim of the lidless can. A few galvanized pails, and a few inexpensive mixing bowls always find a use in the pottery work shop. An assortment of the heavier type elastic bands may be made by cutting cross sections from a discarded inner tube. A wedging board is always desirable; it consists primarily of a shallow box like a cream cheese box filled with plaster and with a vertical rod at the rear end of the box to which is secured a piece of non-rusting wire, not thinner than 12 gauge. The other end of the wire is fastened tightly and stretched to the front end of the box. The wire then forms the hypotenuse of a right triangle.

A scratch point is helpful in scratching designs in a clay body. Such points are sold under that name by any stationery store and are manufactured by Esterbrook Pen Company. They fit into any pen holder.

Make a strainer by nailing a piece of wire screen to the bottom of a rectangle made of four boards.

Rules for Tools

In order to get the most out of your tools, it is advisable to observe a few simple rules.

1. All wooden tools should be thoroughly wiped with a damp cloth when you are finished using them.

2. All metal tools, bowls, and cans should be thoroughly washed and dried when not in use.

3. All plaster surfaces such as bats and wedging boards, should be kept dry and clean. They may be cleaned by wiping the surface with a damp sponge.

4. Knives, in particular, should be kept sharp.

5. Clay, when not in use, should be covered with either waxpaper or a damp cloth, like preserving cheese. It should be kept in a closed crock or other damp-proof container.

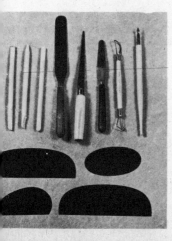

Basic tools for clay work are shown left and right. Included are knives, orange sticks, templates, a wire sculpting tool, sponges and assorted brushes.

How to Make a Wedging Board

A few pieces of scrap wood formed into a box-shape is the first step in constructing a wedging board.

Fasten an upright to the rear piece with nuts and bolts and pour plaster in the box to the very top.

A slight excess of plaster will allow the top of the box to be smoothed off evenly with a straight stick.

The purpose of wedging clay is to eliminate bubbles of air. Level off the surplus plaster from the box.

The wire used as a cutter should be not less than 12 gauge, nichrome, copper or rustproof piano wire.

The wire must be absolutely taut to cut the clay cleanly. Plaster block absorbs the excess moisture.

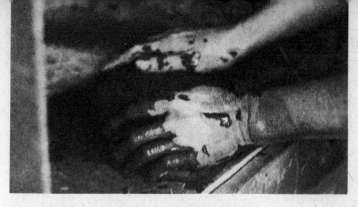

There are a variety of clays that are used for a variety of purposes. Ceramic clays are usually blends of ball clays, talc, flint, feldspar.

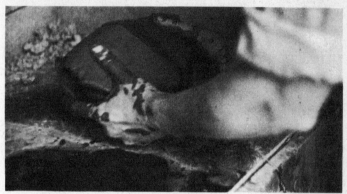

Plasticity is the desirable quality a good modeling clay should have. Malleability means it will absorb grog and flint for firing in kiln.

Types of Clay

There are many different types of clay, employed for various purposes. There are clays used for tennis courts and for marking athletic fields. Clays are used in the formation of fire-resistant sealers, such as fire clay and hearth cement. Clay is used in manufacturing brick for both structural and ornamental uses, and special clays are employed in making porcelain ware which will tolerate the high temperature to which porcelain is exposed. The writer mentions the foregoing only to fire the reader's imagination as to the multiple types and sources of clays. Plasticine is not to be confused with potter's clay or modeling clay. Here we deal only with pottery clays, which are blends of various ball clays, talc, flint, feldspar and other ingredients.

To save the hobbyist the complicated details of preparing his own clay, most of the large wholesalers, such as United Clay Mines and Denver Fire Clay, have prepared a large number of clays either ready mixed to a plastic consistency or ready for the hobbyist to mix with water and wedge to the consistency he requires for his application. For the potter it is less costly to purchase and prepare his plastic body from the clay flour, since purchasing by this means allows the hobbyist full value for his money. (Plastic clay is 25% water.) The only type of raw, pure clay the hobbyist should purchase for starting is a Kaolin, such as Georgia clay, since this has many uses besides being a mill addition to glaze mixture. To mention only a few uses, Kaolin is used in making most glazes. It can be used in making underglazes. It is

Kaolin Analyses

	Georgia Kaolin	No. Car. Kaolin	English China Clay	Florida Kaolin	Alabama Kaolin
Silica	45.30%	46.30%	47.00%	46.30%	44.74%
Alumina	39.14	38.78	37.72	37.70	39.47
Titanium oxide	1.54	0.04	0.15	0.50	1.29
Iron oxide	0.27	0.38	0.96	0.80	0.55
Lime	0.13	0.10	0.19	0.50	0.00
Magnesia	0.04	0.09	0.18	0.00	0.00
Potash	0.15	0.34	1.57	0.20	0.00
Soda	0.10	0.24	0.23	0.00	0.00
Ignition loss	13.71	13.73	12.37	13.70	13.89
	100.38%	100.00%	100.37%	99.70%	99.94%

also used as an ingredient for kiln-wash.

Among the most popular clays for the potter to use are Jordan and Monmouth. These two clays are dark gray in their plastic state but fire to a pink or buff color. Their normal firing range, .02-.06, will accommodate the average potter. They can stand higher temperatures without dunting or melting. All clay can be made to withstand higher temperatures than designated by the addition of finely ground flint to the clay body. This treatment enables the clay to be fired high enough to accommodate a high fired or stone glaze. Clay may also be prepared by placing clay flour and water in a waterproof bag and kneading.

Among the white clays, Whitney and Ebner rank among the popular ceramic bodies. These, too, have a normal range of between cone .02-.06, and fire to a bright white. There is presently a rising demand for natural red clays such as Dalton No. 93 which will tolerate .06 to .01. The higher the fire the darker shade of red the body assumes. There are also several black clays on the market, but these fire only to a mahogany color when fired between .02-.06 (the average hobbyist range). In order for these clays to fire a true black they must be carried up to cone 2. Jordan and Monmouth make good bodies for modeling because of their extreme plasticity. The Whitney is also plastic and fits most glazes which mature at cone .05. On the white surface all glazes fire nearly true, since the clay color, being neutral, does not modify the shade of the glaze. Red clay makes a good base material for sculpturing since it is both plastic and easily malleable. It will readily absorb grog and flint for firing.

Ebner clay makes a good white slip for casting body. Dalton clay No. 35 makes a fairly acceptable red slip. Slip is liquefied clay which has many uses. It is used for cementing together two pieces of clay in their leather state (unfired and not yet dry). Liquid clay (slip) may be applied to both surfaces to be adhered. These surfaces are then firmly pressed together. Particular attention is paid to adhering the edges and, upon drying, the ware becomes one solid mass. Slip made of a colored clay may be applied as decoration.

Make a Plaster Bat

The first step is to make a plaster bat. You employ the pie plate and the plaster for this. Fill any tin or bucket with as much water as the paper pie plate will hold. Into this liquid pour powdered plaster and stir constantly until it reaches the consistency of heavy cream. Pour this liquid plaster quickly into the pie plate and vibrate the plate so as to release any air bubbles. Allow it to set for twenty-four hours and remove the plaster from the paper form. The solid plaster piece you have made is known as a plaster bat and is used as a platform upon which you may work while modeling clay or as a porous surface which will extract excess moisture from a piece of clay upon which you may be working and which is too moist for immediate use.

Data on Ball Clays
RESULTS OF MODULUS OF RUPTURE AND ABSORPTION DETERMINATIONS

Name of clay	Modulus of rupture dried 50 clay—50 flint	Modulus of rupture Cone 5	Modulus of rupture Cone 8	Modulus of rupture Cone 10	Modulus of rupture Cone 12	Semi porcelain Modulus of rupture Cone 8	Per cent absorption Cone 8
English ball clay No. 1	376	958	1926	2473	3271	4108	11.8
English ball clay No. 2	375	937	1527	2300	2467	3783	11.3
English ball clay No. 12	568	1085	1424	2730	3066	4687	9.1
Whiteway ball clay	446	911	1178	2744	2898	4470	9.5
English ball clay No. 90	441	1059	1256	2095	2533	5055	8.8
Pikes ball clay	381	1331	1872	2905	3360	4387	7.2
Superior ball clay	563	885	1077	1572	2561	3788	8.9
Kentucky ball clay No. 4	372	845	999	1513	1982	4118	9.9
Tennessee ball clay No. 5	478	702	947	2135	2104	4854	8.4
No. 25 blue ball clay	403	868	1673	2375	3297	4361	9.5
Tennessee ball clay No. 11	293	682	1004	1447	2355	3748	12.1
Dorset ball clay	492	1333	1502	2184	2844	4396	10.5
Kentucky ball clay No. 10	223	439	844	1121	1620	3671	11.6
English ball clay No. 11	396	1002	1668	2290	3332	4031	10.0
Fayles ball clay	347	1169	1664	2798	2871	4207	9.5
Grindley ball clay	427	913	1320	2518	3207	4568	9.3
Great Beam ball clay	454	1011	1649	2682	3207	4335	10.9
Tennessee ball clay No. 3	327	554	811	1576	1992	3500	11.9
Tennessee ball clay No. 10	...	587	825	1785	1893	2564	13.8
M. & M. English ball clay	384	994	1857	2558	2800	4194	10.7
Tennessee ball clay No. 9	...	625	810	1440	2048	4212	10.6

Compiled by Bureau of Standards.

How to Make a Plaster Bat

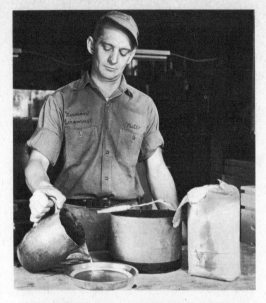

A plaster bat is a slab used in clay work and is easily made. First, fill up a pie pan with water.

Pour the water from the pan into a container and add builder's plaster to heavy cream consistency.

After stirring thoroughly to make sure that lumps and bubbles are removed, mix is ready for pouring.

Pour the plaster slowly into the pie pan. If right amount of plaster has been mixed, pan should fill.

Next, vibrate pan to allow air bubbles to surface, then smooth off the excess plaster to make bat flat.

When the plaster has had time to dry completely, it is removed from pan. This is your working surface.

Ingredients of clay slip are clay flour, water, sodium silicate and sodium carbonate. Scale, measuring cup and bucket are required for preparing the mixture.

Slip

Slip is a mixture of clay and water, or clay, water and other chemicals added to produce certain definite effects.

The water and clay form of slip is used as a mending material to join two pieces of plastic or leather-hard clay. In performing such an operation it is advisable to make your slip of the same material of which you are making your ware, since this type of repair for joining will be invisible when the piece has been dried and fettled. Should you prepare slip of white clay and use it as a mending material on a red or buff clay the repair would be permanently visible.

A slip made of these same ingredients may be used as a decorating slip, provided that the slip is formed from a different color clay from the piece being decorated or is stained with body stain. It is necessary, however, to be sure that the piece you slip-decorate is no drier than in its leathery stage. If this piece is too moist the slip will tend to soften the object being so decorated. If the piece to be decorated is dry, the slip will not adhere and will chip away.

First step in slip making is to pour water into the slip mixer. Then the rest of ingredients are added.

The mixing machine is kept running as components are blended. Pour clay flour to keep dust down.

Slips containing other chemicals utilize that group of chemicals known as deflocculants. In everyday language, a deflocculant is a "water wetter." By this is meant a means of making water so much "wetter" that a small quantity will perform the function of a larger quantity. For example, in order to make ten pounds of clay flour sufficiently fluid for the consistency required for casting, it would be necessary to mix this clay flour with ten pounds of water. By starting with 4½ pounds of water and adding ½ ounce of deflocculant to it, ten pounds of clay becomes as fluid as though there were ten pounds of water mixed with the clay. ●

Things You can Easily Make with Clay

A variety of ceramic objects, both decorative and useful, can reward the clay worker's skill. Above are lamps and a figurine. Jars, pitchers and drinking cups are shown below. Many ceramists sell their ware as a profitable sideline.

Forming an Object with Clay

The impulse to shape clay is a natural one, but give it direction by learning the basic construction techniques.

A cooky cutter is used to cut out a design from clay "dough" and is adhered to a square vase by slip.

EVERY human finds pleasure in handling plastic clay.

If you have bought clay flour to start, put it into a pan with water. Stir thoroughly and allow it to settle. This may take overnight. Pour off excess water and the muddy lump at the bottom is your plastic body. Place this on a plaster bat to draw off the excess water. When your lump of clay has the consistency of putty, throw it forcibly upon your wedging board. Pick it up, cut it across the wire, slap the two pieces one upon the other and repeat the process. After a few repetitions the clay is wedged and ready to work. The simplest form to make for a start is a shallow bowl or vessel. This is easily formed by rolling a ball approximately 7″ in diameter, cutting the ball in half, flattening the bottom slightly on each piece, and allowing these two half balls or shells to rest on your plaster bats. Keep scraping the walls and bottom until they are between ⅛″ and ¼″ in thickness. You may reshape the shell to any shape you desire. This is a free form.

Designs and Shapes

You may, if you wish, use a cooky cutter to cut out a design on a piece of clay which has been rolled out ⅛" thick. To do this, lay a piece of clay on the reverse side of a piece of oilcloth. Use your rolling pin to roll out the clay to the proper thickness. Cut out design with cooky cutter and apply slip on one side of the piece you have cut out. Apply slip to the surface of your vessel where you are going to apply your cooky cutter. Press together gently, but firmly, work edges together and pay particular attention to the contact between the body and the applique at the edges. The applique will become an integral part of your vessel. Now fettle your ware (see page 38) and allow it to dry in preparation for firing.

To form a leaf dish, roll out your clay as before on the wrong side of the oilcloth. Lay a large grape, oak, or maple leaf on the flattened clay. Use a toothpick to score the outline of the leaf. Remove leaf and, using your potter's knife, cut the outline through the clay so that you may pick up your clay leaf. Score the veins into the clay leaf. Curl up the edges and let the piece dry slowly. This type of work will provide inspiration for developing your own original creative forms, from simple objects all around you.

To make a saucer, cut a circle 6" in diameter. Place a drinking glass in the center of the circle. (Note: where glass and clay meet, make sure that contiguous surfaces are Vaseline-greased to prevent sticking.) The drinking glass should be 2½-3" in diameter. Invert so that the center of your circle is supported fully. The edges will droop downward. Shape by hand and let dry. In all of the foregoing we have dealt with making simple pieces. These pieces will require smoothing off or fettling to remove fingerprints and other irregularities. The fettling may be done with a moist sponge or knife while the piece is in its

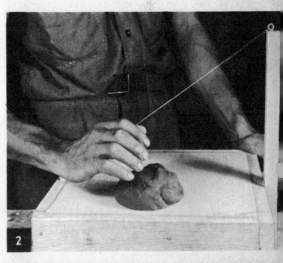

1 To draw off excess water from a lump of clay, place it for a period atop your plaster bat.

2 Before shaping, throw the clay forcibly on the wedging board a few times to render plastic.

3 Cut the clay in half on the wedging wire as a means of making it free of air-bubbles inside.

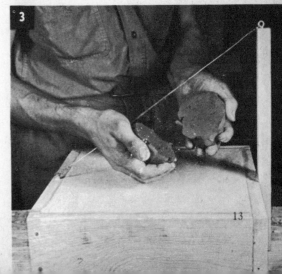

13

To shape a small bowl, start with a sphere of clay about 7" in diameter and cut in half with a knife.

Use a spoon to scoop out the clay from the middle. Don't discard scraps. They are perfectly re-usable.

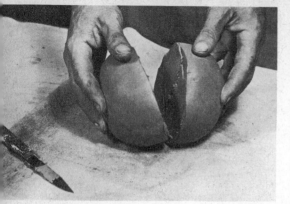

Work and shape the clay until it begins to take the desired form. If it starts to dry, wet your fingers.

The palm of the hand is used to flatten the sides of the bowl, if desired. Other hand gives support.

Common Impurities Found in Water

Mineral Matter	Suspended	Clay Silt		
	Dissolved	Producing Hardness	Silica Iron Alumina Magnesium Calcium	Carbonates Bicarbonates (Temporary)
		Not Producing Hardness	Sodium Potassium	Chlorides Sulphates Nitrates Oxides Hydroxides (Permanent)
Free acids (Sulphuric, etc.)				
Organic Matter	Suspended	Bacteria Animal and vegetable forms such as algae and organisms		
	Dissolved	Soil and vegetable leachings Various materials of organic origin such as sewage and waste		
Gases	Carbon dioxide Oxygen or air Hydrogen sulphide Other gases			

Grady, Ceramic Industry, March, 1935.

A leaf dish is a popular design. Roll out clay to thickness you want, then press leaf into surface.

Cut around the edge of the leaf with a knife, then lift the surplus clay away. Do not include the stem.

Work on oilcloth so that clay can be lifted up. Note that one hand is under cloth, other handles the clay.

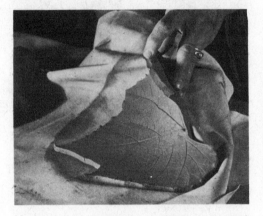

Transfer the clay to your plaster bat. At this point it should be in leather state, firm enough to shape.

leather stage, or with sandpaper or steel wool when the piece has dried thoroughly. In either event when the piece is dry and fettled, remove all excess dust with a damp sponge. You may, if you wish, use your scratch point for cutting a design into your ware. You may incise a design into the inner or exterior surface of your piece. The customary first design is a simple form, such as initials or a star, or a heart. These may be scratched into the ware either when the ware is leather hard or stone dry. Flowers may easily be made by rolling balls of clay in the hand. Balls should be the size of peas for smaller flowers or the size of marbles for larger ones.

Each ball should then be flattened by slapping the hands together with the ball of clay between them. When twenty such pieces have been made, join them together with slip in the shape of flower petals. Make leaves for the flower in the same manner as the leaf dish. For the pistil push a small bit of clay through a strainer and scrape off the bits of strained clay from

With corners turned up to form the dish, support the shape with small balls of clay until it dries hard.

A sawed log effect for a flower holder makes highly decorative item. With spatula, cut ends diagonally.

A spoon is used to scoop out the clay in the center leaving walls of the "log" not more than ¼" thick.

Flatten the piece on the bottom to keep from rolling then score with boxwood tool for a bark-like effect.

Fettling, or cleaning, is done with a smooth tool to eliminate the rough edges and complete the surface.

under the strainer, placing them in the center of the petals, affixing them with a drop of slip.

Many decorative designs are made by rolling out clay, then cutting squares into the shape of 6"x6" tiles and applying (applique) flowers or embossed initials on the tile surface. Religious emblems in particular are popularly constructed in this manner.

Plants and garden bowls are always to be desired, particularly if they resemble parts of the garden. For example, roll a large piece of clay into the shape of a log. Cut both ends of the roll to resemble either the chopping marks of a hatchet or a straight cut of a saw. Flatten the top and bottom slightly and hollow out the interior. Use your boxwood tools to score the outer surface to resemble the bark of a tree. Allow to dry, and fettle.

Doll house furniture has great appeal and is easy to make. Of particular use is a miniature sink, toilet, and tub since in life size these objects are also made of the clay you are using.

Many of the objects you can make are salable to local merchants.

Construction Methods

One of the ancient methods of construction of simple forms which is widely used today is the slab method. This method consists primarily of rolling the clay to uniform thickness and, with a sharp knife, cutting the slabs to form the bottom, sides and ends of a simple shape. These slabs must be permitted to dry slightly before they are handled since in their plastic stage they will warp or bend too freely.

As soon as they have lost some of their plasticity the sides and the ends should be erected upon the base and slip used as the adhesive to join all contiguous surfaces. A piece of this nature must not be allowed to dry too quickly as it will warp very badly if subjected to rapid drying.

There are three standard methods of forming objects with clay. It is necessary to have standard methods since the methods with which we have already dealt would apply only to small objects. In making a large piece it is necessary actually to construct your piece much as a builder would erect a house. He begins with a base and works up the sides slowly, making certain

The slab method is one of the oldest ways of clay modeling. Roll out clay on back side of oilcloth.

To make a box-shaped piece, cut a cardboard bottom and sides, lay them out on the clay for size.

Cut out the clay sections with knife, and assemble them on a plaster bat or plywood square, as shown.

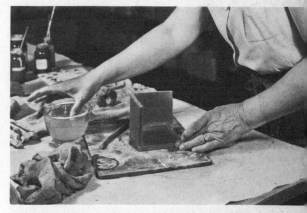

Clay slip is the adhesive used in joining the parts of the box. Keep some water handy for wetting clay.

For a perfect joint, all areas to be fitted should be coated with slip. Clay should be leather-state.

Strengthen joints by using coiled clay in corners. This technique also calls for liberal use of slip.

A wooden stick is used to impress coiled clay into corners. If skillfully done, no traces will remain.

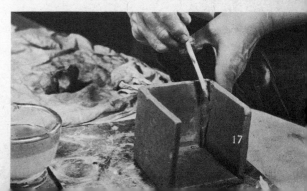

17

Another way to make a box is to square off a bottom and build up the sides with small coils made of clay.

Slip must be used as each coil is added. When walls are in position, smooth them out with your fingers.

that each portion of his wall rests securely upon the section or sections beneath it and that those sections rest securely upon the base.

Let us deal with the simplest and most ancient method. Take a small piece of clay and lay it on the underside of a piece of oilcloth, making sure that the oilcloth is fully supported on a table top or other smooth surface. With the palm of the hand, gently roll the clay back and forth until a long, thin, tubular shaped piece, about the thickness of a large worm, has been extruded. You have formed what is technically known as a coil. Take one end of the coil and hold it firmly down with one hand while winding the balance of the coil in concentric circles around the end you are holding in position. In this method you are forming the base of the object you are building. You continue constructing coils and wind them in the same manner in which you started the piece. Should cracks develop in the winding it may indicate that the clay has not been properly wedged, or that the clay is too dry. Correct these conditions and if neither of these remedies cure the condition then the clay is known to be "short." This is also applicable in pie baking and may be more readily understandable when compared to pie dough which is too rich. The simplest remedy under these conditions would be to work your piece as though it were not short and then make a thick slip (clay and water) and apply this mixture with a brush over any and all blemishes while the piece is still plastic.

In joining the coils it is best to slit the beginning of the new coil in a diagonal, presenting as large a surface for adhesion as is conveniently possible. Coat both surfaces so treated with slip and press firmly together. When the base is completely formed and constructed to the size you desire, you will have made a piece resembling a hooked rug. This base need not be circu-

lar. If you desire an elliptical shape, the coils would be thicker in the direction of the long diameter and thinner in the direction of the short diameter. A square base may also be constructed of coils. Over the surface of the base apply slip with a soft brush. This will seal the joints of the coils and provide firm adherence.

In constructing the sides, the coil is firmly secured on top of the coil beneath it, again using slip much as a builder uses mortar. It is not necessary to raise your sides in a true vertical. The sides may bulge outwardly for some distance of the rise and then may slope inwardly, much like a pitcher. Depending upon the size of the piece, it may be necessary to halt your construction of a large piece and allow it to dry slightly (to a leathery consistency) in order to give it sufficient strength to support the weight of succeeding coils. In the event you find this necessary, it is advisable to moisten thoroughly the point at which you commence your next step of the work, as clay which has dried to a leathery consistency will not adhere to a plastic section of clay. This may be done by putting a damp cloth on the top coil.

Should you find the ridges created by the exterior surface undesirable, you may work the ridges down by applying slip to the surface of these ridges and rubbing gently with the thumbs. This will wear down the curvature of the ridges and fill in the sections between which the coils are joined.

If you are going to construct a symmetrical piece it is a good idea to cut out a template made from a piece of cardboard so that you may, from time to time, check the symmetry of the piece while it is being built. When the piece is entirely finished, it should be sanded smooth unless you want the coil marks to show, in which event the sanding is done only to remove the slip marks.

Greater strength may be obtained in building a piece by using irregular pieces.

For best use of the coil method, a round piece is suggested. Make template for bottom, cut clay out.

Applying slip to all coils and the bottom, form the base firmly. The coils should be about ½″ diameter.

The coils are rolled out by hand and should be in a slightly leathery stage for maximum working ease.

To join the coils as you build, stroke them up and down all the way around, pressing them together.

of clay which are put together with slip just as a builder constructs a stone wall of irregularly sized rocks.

In this type of construction, if smooth surfaces are desired, they may be had by trimming the uneven edges while the piece is in its leather stage by using a fettling knife, or by waiting until the piece is thoroughly dried and sanding the surfaces with either steel wool or sandpaper. •

Cracks in Clay

Occasionally, cracks will appear in a piece of clay ware after it has dried. While the cause may be in the clay itself, the trouble generally lies in incorrect building of the piece. Cracks are almost certain to appear when coils have been imperfectly welded.

To mend such cracks, dampen the area carefully until it is once again plastic. Dig a groove where the crack appeared and fill with a fresh coil of clay. Gently work the clay in until it has melded with the moistened surface.

A template is used to see that the clay bowl is the same height all around. Then finish shaping it.

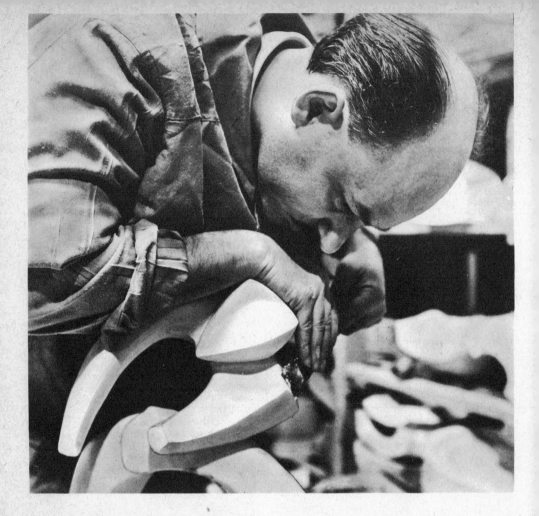

Sculpting

Here is the true test of your clay-working and artistic craftsmanship.

Modeling tools are necessary for effective sculpting after preliminary shaping. Below is a selection of wooden tools that can be purchased or made. At right: five basic tools every sculptor should own.

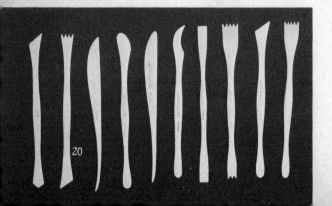

SMALL WIRE TOOL—ABOUT 4¾" LONG

WIRE TOOL—ABOUT 7½" LONG

HARDWOOD TOOL—ABOUT 7" LONG

HARDWOOD TOOL—ABOUT 5" LONG

HARDWOOD TOOL—ABOUT 5" LONG

20

IN SCULPTING, you will find each of the previous steps helpful in aiding you to develop a flair for this form of ceramic work.

In preparation for sculpting it will be necessary to consider the different problems that will project themselves in this type of work. The size of the piece to be formed will, of necessity, have a direct bearing on the type of material to be used.

In forming a large piece it is necessary to have the body of the clay plastic enough to work and yet firm enough not to squash down or dunt from its own weight. In a small piece not too much attention will be necessary to these considerations since the weight of a small piece is not too vital a factor. Most prepared clays for sculpture work are reinforced with other materials, which serve two purposes. One is to prevent dunting and the other is to prevent cracking or warping during the drying process. The principal material added to the clay used for this process is grog. Grog is actually clay which has been fired and crushed. This crushed matter is then passed through various sized sieves and packaged according to size. Grog for sculpting may be as coarse as a No. 10 mesh; this would be equal to a fairly coarse gravel, or it may be as fine as a No. 30 mesh, which would be a little bit finer than sea sand. The grade to be used and the quality should be based on the size of the piece you are going to construct. A larger piece will require more and coarser grog proportionately than will a small piece. Percentage of grog when mixed with clay may range as much as 50% of your plastic body.

21

Grog is mixed with clay to prevent cracking and/or warping in sculptured pieces. To make grog, put a piece of unglazed, fired bisque ware in a burlap bag and crush it to bits with flat side of hammer.

Next, place the clay on the back side of a piece of oilcloth and make it flat with a rolling pin. A mass of clay should be small enough to be readily wedged. Proportion of grog should be above 15%.

How to Use Grog

Grog is obtainable from most brickyards. These yards crush up their breakage and sell this broken material according to the size. You may prepare your own grog by crushing up any clay object which has been fired but unglazed. This is best done by putting a piece of bisque ware into a heavy canvas or burlap bag, placing the bag upon a rock or other hard surface and striking repeated hammer blows against the middle of the bag, thereby crushing the contents within the bag between the blows of the hammer on one side and the underlying surface on the other side.

In mixing the grog with clay it is advisable first to approximate the size of the piece you are going to create and its weight. Weigh out the proportionate amount of grog between 15% and 50%. Divide your mass of clay into sections small enough to be wedged individually. In front of each piece of clay, put the portion of grog you are going to use. This will aid in mixing your materials. Roll out the piece of clay on the reverse side of your piece of oil-cloth. Make this piece ¼" thick and scatter grog over the entire surface; fold in half and roll the plastic clay in its own pile of grog. Repeat this same process with the same piece until its own pile of grog is completely imbedded in the clay. Perform the same operation with the remaining clay and grog. Wedge this material thoroughly (see chapter one for wedging).

Another method of mixing grog clay is to mix the clay flour and grog together thoroughly in their dry state in the proportions required for the size piece you are going to form. To this dry mixture add about 25% water by volume. Stir with a strong wood stick and cover tightly; allow to stand at least 24 hours before using. If more water is required, add it before wedging. If the clay should be too moist, dry it out on a plaster bat until it is plastic, and then wedge it.

As at left, sprinkle the grog over the rolled-out clay. The clay should be about a quarter of an inch thick and the grog should be placed over the whole surface. If you desire, buy grog at brickyards.

Press the grog into the plastic clay with rolling pin, moving it back and forth vigorously. Another method of mixing in grog is to take clay flour and add grog to it, then reduce the batch with water.

It is important that the grog be evenly distributed throughout the clay. To this end, fold the clay on itself, as at left, and repeat the flattening out process over and over, using rolling pin technique.

Pounding with the fist is a good way to help work the grog into the clay. The grade and quality used depend on the size of the piece to be sculpted. A larger object will require more and coarser grog.

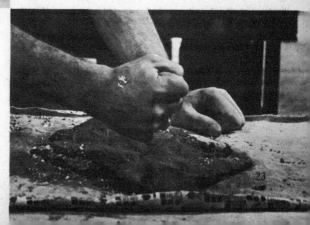

23

A substantial amount of detail work enters into the modeling of figurines. Suggestion, rather than slavish accuracy, however, should guide you in facial features and hair, as these will be painted in later.

Molding Figurines

Among the most suitable types of clay for sculpture work, particularly if it is to assume fairly large proportions, are terra cotta, Jordan and Monmouth.

In making a figure from a solid piece of clay it is advisable to determine first the general outline and in so doing divide the figure into its most prominent and least prominent parts, based on volume. For example, one of the most popular figures is the figurine of an old woman in native costume with a bundle of balloons over her shoulder. In considering the construction of the figure the most prominent part would be the lower portion with its billowing skirt topped by a broad waist. The second most prominent part of this figure is the torso, which includes two arms, a short bull-like neck, and a proportionately small, round head. The outline of these parts can be made from lumps of clay barely shaped, and if the clay is very plastic, no slip will be required in joining the sections. When the outline proportion is partly shaped, the lumps of clay are assembled. Their mass should be placed on a plaster bat which has been soaked in water.

The general shape will be larger than the finished piece, since clay will be carved

off in forming the piece and since the piece will shrink as it dries.

With a wire tool, outline the skirt. Take off and add clay to obtain the right outline. Revolve the piece frequently while you are working so that you may view it from all directions and work the front and rear together. Observe from all angles until you are satisfied that you have achieved what was in your mind's eye when you began. If you have difficulty in visualizing the folds of the skirt, it would be a good idea to form a wire circle approximately the size of the waist. Drape a piece of soft cloth around the wire circle, holding it up and noticing the way the folds of cloth drape. This can be used as a model for you to copy the folds of the skirt. In forming the torso, define sharply the indentations which will represent the division between the body proper and the arms. Be sure to outline the suggestion of the bosom as it would appear under a coarse fabric forming the bodice of a peasant costume. For the face and head start with oval or egg shape and fashion, with suggestion rather than accuracy, nose, lips, eyes, and other facial details. Remember that these features will probably be painted in later.

Such details as a head scarf will eliminate the necessity of defining the ears, neck cords, and even parts of the neck line.

Do not let the figure dry out while you are working on it. In between your working sessions, cover the piece with a damp cloth or plastic material. Keep the piece either in an old icebox or under a crock or a can.

When the piece is entirely completed, but still in its leather stage, use a spoon or a knife to hollow out the solid object. It should be hollowed out to a wall thickness of between ½″ and ¾″.

In order to eliminate the necessity of hollowing the piece, you may, if you wish, make a wad of newspaper and wrap your starting clay around the wad of paper. Proceed as directed to sculpt your piece, shaping it as explained in the foregoing paragraphs. When this piece is fired in the kiln, the paper will burn out, leaving the piece hollow. A later chapter covers firing preparations and techniques.

Large pieces may also be sculptured from outlines or forms built up by the coil method.

In making shapes with elongated, unsupported areas, like the barrel of a horse or a dachshund, it is wise to construct your piece on an armature. An armature is a device made of supporting material such as wood, or wood combined with wire or paper, upon which clay forms are supported while being modeled. If you use a wooden armature it will be necessary to expose a portion of the armature so that it may be burned out in the bisque firing. If, on the other hand, you use a wire armature, it should be removed before the firing. If it cannot be removed, the piece should not be fired. •

Examples of the sculptor's art show wide diversity of subject matter and treatment available to the hobbyist, from portrait-busts to whimsical animals.

Molds and Mold Making

**The one-piece or two-piece methods are equally desirable
for production in quantity of the shapes you want to make.**

THE simplest form of mold is a plaster press mold. Let us assume that you want to reproduce a certain type of button or ornament. Obtain or make a small box which will be six or seven times larger than the form or button you want to reproduce.

Paint the object which you want to reproduce with a liquid soap either made by boiling the waste ends of any of your household soap with water or using a bottle of green soap. After the object is thoroughly soap-painted, mix a solution of potter's plaster and water. When this has reached the consistency of heavy cream, pour it into the box, and shake or vibrate the box to release all air bubbles. When the plaster has begun to set, but before it has become solid, push the button or ornament into the soft plaster but do not allow the back to go below the plaster surface. When the plaster has set up you will have no difficulty removing the ornament from the plaster because of the soaped surface. This soap material is known as a separator. Remove the box from around the plaster. After the plaster has dried thoroughly it may be used in the following manner: a piece of clay is pressed into the indentation. The outside surface is smoothed off. Wait a few minutes; moisture from the plastic clay will be absorbed by the plaster of the mold and the clay will begin to shrink slightly. Invert the plaster mold and tap gently. The clay reproduction will fall out.

Materials required for mold making include a pencil, paint brushes, scraper, clay, liquid soap and a box shape. Below, the two halves of a two-piece mold for a vase are flanked at right by the original model and at left by the casting made from it.

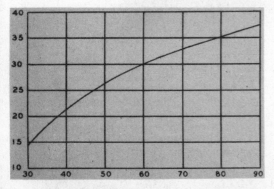

Curve shows effect of consistency on water absorption of gypsum plaster in pounds of water per 100 lbs. plaster. Absorption per cu. ft. is shown left.

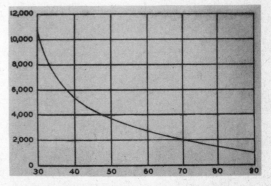

With figures in left column representing dry compressive strength (psi) graph shows consistency of gypsum plaster in pounds of water per 100 pounds.

First step in making the one-piece mold is to pour plaster into water through strainer or fine-mesh sieve.

Continue pouring, as below, till all the plaster you intend to make has been added before you start to mix.

The One-Piece Mold

In making a one-piece mold it is easier to make your mold around either the piece you are going to copy or from a clay shape you have designed. The first step would be to find or construct a pan or box of cardboard, metal, or wood large enough to accommodate the outside of the plaster mold. Use any separator to paint the inside of your vessel. This will keep the plaster, with which you will make the mold, from sticking. In this case your separator may be a grease-like vaseline, a heavy oil, a coat of paraffin, or liquid soap.

For example, if you desire to reproduce a mixing bowl, place the shape you are going to duplicate with the rim or top of bowl down. Make sure that the rim meets the bottom of the vessel and that the sides of your box or vessel into which you will pour plaster are higher than the bowl you are going to use as a model for a mold.

Cover your model thoroughly with soap separator. Now prepare your plaster, stir-

When the plaster forms an island in the water it is time to mix. Be certain that it is lump-free.

Box shape has been firmly placed on smooth clay. Put in form top down and paint it with separator.

Plaster is then poured over the form. Keep spout low so as not to splatter and cause air bubbles.

Pour slowly and with care, making sure that there is enough plaster covering the bottom of the form.

After the plaster has completely set, pry the box apart and remove the entire piece from the base.

Actually, the box shape need not be taken entirely apart. Loosening it slightly makes it removable.

ring thoroughly until it has reached the consistency of cream. Pour your plaster into the vessel completely around the outside of the model you are reproducing and also continue to pour plaster until the bottom of the bowl you are fashioning is covered by at least one inch of plaster. Pour carefully to prevent air bubbles. If you feel that there is a tendency for the model to slip from position, you may hold it in place by pushing the thumb downward against the bottom of the bowl. When you feel the plaster beginning to set, remove the thumb and fill the impression quickly and smooth over. As soon as the plaster has set, knock the mold out of the vessel in which it was poured. The matrix, or form, which is now imbedded in the plaster should come out easily if there has been adequate separator used on the model. If air bubbles appear on the inside of the mold, these may be patched with a little plaster and water.

If you are going to reproduce a vessel which you have made of clay, your model should be in its leathery stage. Pour a ¼" slip in the pan. Place your model on this slip, as it will begin to set at once, and keep your model from moving. No separator will be required. Pour your plaster the same as before. It will not be necessary to hold the piece in place. Remove the plaster mold from the vessel as before and, with a nut pick or fettling knife, carefully remove the moist clay or slip from the mold. You will in all probability destroy your model. Be careful in removing the pieces of clay so that you do not mar the mold. Make sure that the piece you are using as a model has no undercuts.

Now you are ready to take the form out of the mold. It will come out readily if the separator has been applied thoroughly. Lift it without nicking mold.

Below is the finished one-piece mold and the form from which it was made. Examine the mold for imperfections which may be patched with plaster.

Molding Memos

In cleaning a mold, use only a moist sponge. Any other method may damage the plaster.

A mold should be absolutely dry before it is used. Expose it to warm air or an infra-red lamp. Do not bake.

If your mold does not release ware easily, use talcum powder inside, in a thin coat. The powder will show on the clay, but can be easily sponged off.

Do not store molds in a damp place, as this encourages fungi to grow on the plaster.

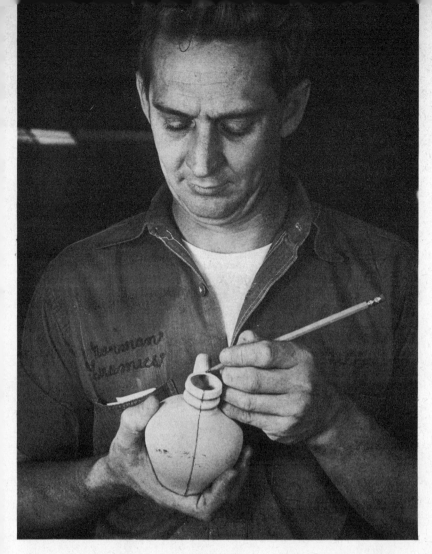

This vase is going to be used as the form for two-piece mold. A pencil or crayon line is drawn along its center, running vertically from top to bottom.

Using a spatula, prepare a recessed area in solid bed of clay to hold the form. Note that pencil line has been made on handle as well as on vase.

The Two-Piece Mold

In making a two-piece mold let us assume that you are going to reproduce a simple lamp base or vase. Examine your sample carefully. If there appear to be no undercuts, lay it upon its side or hold it in a horizontal position so that the respective bottom and top are in either end. Draw a line dividing the model in half, with either a glass-marking crayon or a pencil. This line will run horizontally from the top to the bottom of the model, since the model is lying in a horizontal position. Stop up the mouth of the vessel with a solid wad of clay which should project two inches beyond

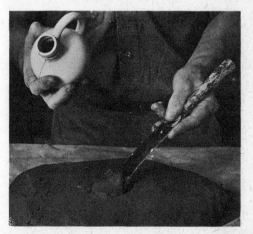

31

The model is centered in the clay. When imbedding the piece be sure clay comes up to the centerline.

The vase opening is stopped with a cork or a lump of clay. Build up to centerline with surplus clay.

Marbles or similar pieces are used as a locking device to secure half of mold with its other half.

The box shape is placed around the form. It should be at least two inches higher than exposed model.

Spread some clay around the edges of the box to prevent plaster from running out when poured.

Now the form and the clay bed is thoroughly coated with separator. Liquid soap is recommended here.

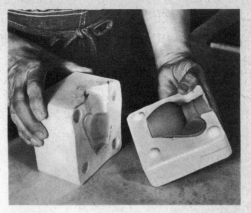

Use separator on inside walls of box, too. Then pour plaster carefully to the very top of the box.

When the plaster hardens you have half the mold. Use this half with box shape to produce the other.

the opening of the model. Imbed this model in a block of clay up to the pencil line. In other words, half of the model will now be imbedded in a clay block. Allow the end of the stopper to project slightly beyond the clay block. Smooth off the surface of the clay absolutely level with the line marked on your model. Build a form around the clay block in which the model is imbedded. The form is built only on four sides, not bottom nor top. The form around the block of clay should be at least two inches higher than any part of the exposed model. The form may be made of transite, linoleum, rubber tile, asphalt tile, or stiff cardboard. Looking down at your form, now, you should see a block of clay surrounded on four sides by a stiff material, either tied or banded together so as to enclose securely the block of clay with the model half embedded.

Using your soap separator, thoroughly cover the inside walls of your form from the block of clay to the top of the wall. Apply your separator on the model. Prepare your plaster as before and pour to the very top of your wall or form. As soon as the plaster has set, remove the walls and remove all clay from the model. Do not remove the form nor the stopper from the mold. You now have half of the plaster mold. Turn the plaster mold over, so that half of the model now projects upward as it did when it was imbedded in clay. Put your walls around the plaster mold the same as you did around the clay; gouge out of the plaster mold, at the solid corners, four hemispheres much like the impression a half of a ¾" marble would make if it had been pressed into the flat surface of the plaster near the corner. Now paint all of the exposed surface with a separator. It is very

important that your soap separator solution should thoroughly cover the exposed plaster model and inside walls of the form. Pour plaster to the height of the walls. When the plaster has set, remove the walls and, using a spatula or dull round-ended knife, pry the two plaster sections apart. Remove the model. Take away the stopper.

You will notice that the indentations or locks which you notched out of the first half of the mold now have their counterpart in male form on the second half of the plaster mold. The clay stopper when removed from the respective holder of the mold will now form the pouring spout through which slip is poured. This mold should dry for several days before it has allowed sufficient porosity to function properly.

The number of pieces or sections used in making a mold are determined strictly by undercuts. An undercut is a part of a model or form where either slip or plaster, in making the model, will form a hook and thereby make it impossible to remove the mold or the cast afterward. In cases like this, separate sections of the plaster mold which can be individually removed overcome this obstacle.

There is also the waste mold method. In this method the making of one form is of paramount importance and the mold is completely destroyed in order to remove the casting. This is done in lieu of making an extremely complex multiple mold and particularly where quantity reproduction is not essential.

Where quantity reproduction is essential and the form is complex, it is simplest to make individual molds of the separate parts and adhere these parts with slip to form the complete complex object. •

Slip Casting

Learn to use this professional way of producing inexpensive, multiple copies of a design from your mold.

IN POURING slip into molds you are following the commercial method of reproducing clay objects in the same form and in appreciable amount. To do this type of work, you will need a mold, fettling knife, assortment of brushes, a sponge, elastic bands and a pitcher for pouring slip. Make sure your mold is absolutely dry. Close it and secure it tightly with heavy rubber bands. Place the mold on a level surface and pour strained slip from a pitcher, or a can with a spout. Do not pause in the pouring action. The flow of slip into the mold must be constant, or otherwise there will be a mark on the ware indicating the cessation of pouring and the point where you continued.

Allow the slip to remain in the mold until it has thickened to not less than ⅛". Then invert the mold and allow the excess slip in liquid form to pour back into the pitcher. Allow the clay which has adhered to the inside of the mold to set until it loses its shine. This process should take about 20 minutes. Remove the rubber bands and rock the mold to loosen the newly formed object from the inner surface of the mold. Carefully pry apart the sections of the mold and your object will be formed.

This ware may be fettled within 15 minutes by the use of a sponge or brush. If it is allowed to become bone dry, it can be fettled with a knife and sandpaper or steel wool.

It is important that the mold be allowed to dry before storing away. If a mold is going to be used repeatedly, the application of talcum powder brushed on the inner surface will be extremely advantageous.

There are several important factors to be observed in slip casting; i.e., if the clay is left too long in the mold, the resultant shrinkage may cause parts of the ware to break, such as the handle of a tea cup. If the mold is too wet it will be unable to extract enough moisture to solidify the slip. If the mold is not tightly bound, the weight of the clay will force the sections apart and your slip will run out from between the crevices.

Care must be used in fettling in order not to efface the individualistic characteristics of the form you are casting.

Preparing Your Casting Slip

Let us examine the possibilities of making a casting slip using clay and water alone. Ten pounds of water and ten pounds of clay mixed thoroughly will make a solution dense enough for casting.

If we pour this solution into a mold it will require probably one half hour of waiting for enough water to be absorbed by the plaster mold so that the part of the clay which touches the mold may solidify. The rigidity which the clay assumes can be attained only when it loses the moisture which kept it fluid.

The next step would be to pour out the excess liquid clay from within the mold and allow the mold to set for further drying. The following step would be to open the mold and allow the piece extracted to set up rigidly.

We started with dry clay, and we doubled the weight with water. By allowing a piece so formed to dry thoroughly we would be extracting our water. Such a severe absorption of water as would take place in the plaster mold or in the open air would in all probability cause very severe cracking and warpage and the shrinkage would be so great that the finished piece would only resemble a miniature.

The second consideration would be that the extreme absorption of fluid by the mold would render the mold useless for several days until the excess water had been evaporated. This would certainly render ceramic mold casting a sorry means of inexpensive multiple production.

In order to overcome these flaws you must understand that the remedy is to

A homemade pitcher for pouring slip can be made by hammering a spout into the lip of a can. This saves having to use one of your better pitchers.

make the water wetter and thereby use less water though still obtaining the same fluidity necessary for a successful and graceful casting. A simple formula which may be adjusted easily by any clay enthusiast is the following: Into any wide-mouthed container larger than a gallon size, pour 4½ pounds of water. Add ½ liquid ounce sodium silicate. Add 1/10 ounce sodium carbonate or barium carbonate. These chemicals may be purchased at your local drugstore (1/10 ounce will be the quantity which will remain on the tip of a fruit knife if it is dipped in a box of sodium or barium carbonate). Stir the ingredients into the water thoroughly; add ten pounds of clay flour. Stir thoroughly and allow to settle for 24 hours. Stir again and strain (a good strainer is a woman's silk stocking).

The longer slip stands, the better it becomes. Aged slip frequently acquires an offensive odor. This odor frequently indicates the aging process induced by bacterial

Strips of rubber from an old inner tube will make strong bands to hold the two parts of your plaster mold well secured.

Table Showing Weight of Solids, Per Cent Water, Per Cent Solids for a Given Slip Weight Per Pint

Weight Per Pint		Oz. Solids Per Pint	Per Cent Water	Per Cent Solids
18	oz.	2.17	87.90	12.10
19	oz.	3.83	79.84	20.16
20	oz.	5.50	72.50	27.50
21	oz.	7.17	65.86	34.14
22	oz.	8.84	59.82	40.18
23	oz.	10.50	54.35	45.65
24	oz.	12.17	49.29	50.71
25	oz.	13.84	44.64	55.36
26	oz.	15.51	40.30	59.70
27	oz.	17.18	36.37	63.63
28	oz.	18.84	32.72	67.28
29	oz.	20.51	29.28	70.72
29½	oz.	21.34	27.66	72.34
30	oz.	22.17	26.10	73.90
30½	oz.	23.00	24.59	75.41
31	oz.	23.84	23.10	76.90
31¼	oz.	24.26	22.37	77.63
31½	oz.	24.67	21.69	78.31
31¾	oz.	25.09	20.95	79.05
32	oz.	25.50	20.31	79.69
33	oz.	27.17	17.67	82.33

action in your slip. This process can be hastened by the addition of ½ cup of a weak solution of gum arabic.

Gum arabic (acacia) may be bought at your local drugstore. A teaspoonful put in a gallon of water, brought to a boil, and then allowed to simmer until all of the gum is dissolved, will provide an adequate solution for your casting slip.

Certain clays, such as Dalton No. 93, red, or Jordan, may require more water. This can be added to your mixture before straining. Your slip, to be proper, should flow off a spoon with the consistency and continuity of honey.

Your slip should be kept in a wooden container or a clay crock and should be kept covered when not in use. It should be thoroughly stirred before each use but not churned rapidly, as this will mix air with the slip and leave little craters in your casting. If you store your slip in a metal container, the liquid content will affect the metal and cause rust motes to adulterate your otherwise clear slip.

Under no conditions deposit your fettlings with your slip as this will spoil the balance of your slip. Fettlings should be stored, and when dry, crushed and treated as clay flour in a preparation of future slip. Slips may be artificially colored with body stains, which are more fully dealt with in a later chapter.

Don't use slip when it is too fresh. The older it is the better. Be sure to strain it, however, before using. Avoid fettlings which may have steel wool in them or abrasives from sandpaper. To age slip artificially, add gum arabic—one pint to fifty pounds of clay flour

With mold held together tightly by rubber bands, a solution of slip is poured in. Consistency should be that of honey and pouring should be done without interruption in order to avoid marks on the casting.

When the slip reaches the top of the mold, let it settle, then add more. Excess slip should be poured off after the slip in the mold has thickened to not less than ⅛ inch. Invert the mold to drain off.

Tip the mold from side to side to make sure that excess is removed, as mold may have arms or indentations that might create pockets for surplus slip. Clay inside mold should set until it loses shine.

In producing a casting from clay slip, the plaster mold absorbs the moisture from the slip, building up a wall on the inside of the mold. Test the thickness of this wall with a knife, as at left, above. If the wall is thick enough, remove the rubber bands carefully from the mold, as in the center photo, and shake it a few times (right) to insure even distribution and help loosen the casting from the mold.

The first step in taking apart the mold is to remove the lid. Pry away the clay that has formed in the opening (left above) using care so that the casting itself is not pulled out of shape. The lid may now be removed (center) in order to speed the setting process. Before prying apart the mold, be sure that the slip has reached the leather stage. A flat knife or spatula may then be inserted between halves.

With the mold loosened, pull apart gently with the hands, keeping an eye on the casting to see that it has not adhered to both of the inside walls. Usually it will stick to one wall only and should be laid down so that it rests on that side (center photo). A casting is removed from the mold by tilting over and letting it drop out of its own accord. If it sticks, don't force out. Let it harden a longer time.

Fettling

No matter how well a piece of ware is constructed it will look crude unless the surface is finished. Be sure to use proper tools, materials.

FETTLING is the term used for describing the operation of removing unevenness, mold marks, fingerprints or other irregularities from a piece of ware.

In considering methods, it is first necessary to take into account the condition and type of the ware and decide which method shall be applicable.

A knife shaped like a sharp kitchen paring knife with a blade slightly longer and thinner and having a sharp point, is suitable as a fettling knife. Such a knife should be of extremely flexible steel and should have a good cutting edge. The handle should fit comfortably in the palm of the hand. The tool should be light enough so

38

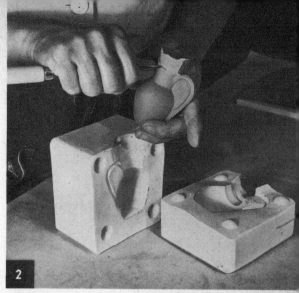

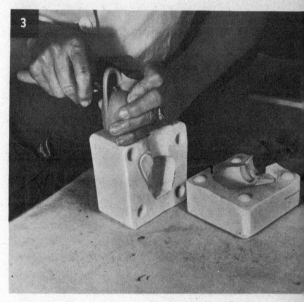

1   After carefully removing the piece from its mold it is ready for fettling. It should be in a leather stage, not too damp and not too brittle. Almost all ware requires finishing.

2   The preliminary fettling should be done with a knife. Remove all excess clay, being sure that such spots as the inside of the handle and the top of the vase are deftly treated.

3   When using a knife or spatula on your ware, hold it gently but firmly in your hand so it doesn't slip, but support your hand, in turn, so that arm movements do not spoil piece.

that nimble and dexterous fingers may delicately work a piece of clay.

A spatula found among most kitchen tools is also an unusually useful fettling edge, since its edges are straight and the blade exceedingly flexible, yet strong and well-balanced. There are many such scraping tools for special application.

Sandpaper or garnet paper of the finest quality is a necessity for smoothing out an uneven surface. Frequently, fine household steel wool is used too as a method of evening out large irregularities or thinning out too thick a wall. The sharpness of steel wool makes an impression more rapidly than most other abrasives.

Probably the most universally used tool for fettling is a sponge. Sponges come in all shapes and sizes. The most common of these is an elephant ear. This is a sponge of very fine texture similar to a facial sponge, not thicker than ½″ to ¾″ and approximately 4″ to 5″ across.

Each of the foregoing tools, however, have advantages and disadvantages which must be considered before using them. The knife, for example, is a fine tool with which to remove jagged thin edges which are left on a piece of cast ware by the mold. If, however, the jagged piece to be removed is coarse and heavy, the knife may cut too deeply or cause a break in the ware. Square

Nimble and dexterous fingers are important in all fettling operations, and tools should be light and delicate without noticeable weight or imbalance.

A sponge is considered a most useful fettling and shaping device, particularly when claywork is in a plastic stage. Sponges are used at start and finish.

After the major part of the waste clay has been removed, a brush dipped in water will serve to take mold marks away. Don't make ware too moist.

A fine file is also a handy tool and is employed to supplement a knife. Some ceramists prefer rubbing with fingers, as skin offers some abrasive action.

Many mold makers use garnet paper, as at left, to fettle. For small figures it should be of very fine grades. Large ware is fettled with coarser types.

or straight surfaces may be cut or scraped by the knife method, but a rounded surface may be ruined by the straight cut of a knife blade. If a piece of ware is fettled while moist or leather-hard, the coarse trimming may be safely done by knife and the finer work by rubbing lightly over the surface to be finished with a fine, moist sponge. If the ware is bone dry, it may be scraped moderately, by spatula or knife or suitable scraper, to remove the coarse irregularities, and then the fine finish may be completed by use of sandpaper or steel wool.

Both sandpaper and steel wool are apt to leave deposits of foreign matter on the surface of the ware which will cause the glaze to magnify these blemishes. Therefore, it is important, when finishing a piece, to remove all such deposits by carefully brushing with a dry, soft varnish brush and then wiping carefully with a damp sponge.

A piece of ware may be fettled in its wet plastic state by the use of a moist elephant ear sponge. This is often considered the safest time and manner to fettle, since damages to the ware may be easily repaired while in the plastic stage, and a sponge is more easily adapted to the contour of your piece than any steel knife or abrasive surface. In addition, since the sponge is used in final treatment after all other methods, it follows that the use of the sponge alone is a time saver on this tedious but necessary part of ceramic work. ●

Steel wool is sometimes used, but care must be taken to see that it does not leave bits in the ceramic ware.

Decorating Your Ceramic Ware

Learn the art of transforming bare clay shapes into objects of enduring value and beauty.

At right, a design has been incised with a knife. This piece has been cast and still needs trimming.

ALL types of wonderful designs can be made by slip painting, or engobe work, as the application of a clay slip upon another piece of clay is called. One color placed over another color and shaded with highlights of blending shades create a thing of beauty when glazed to cover the bodies and render the various colors into a unit. Many interesting and attractive designs can also be made by covering the body of a piece of ware with one or more engobes and scratching a design through the engobe to the original surface color of the clay body of your ware.

Such scratched designs can be left raw or filled in with still another engobe. Useful tools for this work are a scratch point (sgraffito knife)—a point resembling a steel nib, fitting into any regular pen holder—a darning needle, a long hat pin, a quill from a chicken. All these make extremely useful tools for cutting the engobe in order to score a design. An assortment of water color brushes No. 1, No. 4, No. 10, and a ¼" and ½" varnish brush are helpful in applying engobe. A sharp knife with a fine point will aid in making deeper cuts into your ware.

Another interesting method of design is to fill a small syringe with a rubber bulb and a fairly long (2½" by 4") nozzle with engobe and form a design or pattern by squeezing the rubber bulb to force out a thin line of engobe through the nozzle. The design is formed much as a pastry chef squeezes out his tube of icing sugar on a cake to form initials and flowers. An irregular criss-cross pattern can be used this way and the alternate areas filled in with various colors. This type of work, when complete and glazed, resembles mosaic design, since the irregular lines squeezed from the syringe form the boundaries of each of the additional colors. The syringe is known in clay craft as a "slip tracer." Delicately embossed flowers and leaves can be placed on the most simple pattern by means of a slip tracer.

Wedgwood is a form of slip painting, or

slip coloring. The easiest way to produce an attractive wedgwood effect is to purchase or make casting slip in several different colors.

Select a mold, preferably with a cameo or floral design. Paint with a brush the portion of the mold which has the design. Use one color casting slip for this work. Now fill the mold with another color casting slip and treat as you would in any slip casting work. When your piece comes out of the mold the two colors of slip will have become one piece of clay but their separate colors will remain distinctive and apart from each other. Many seemingly impossible designs are so formed.

It is also possible and desirable to pour a decorative design in one color slip and pour a simple design (such as an ash tray or cigarette box) in another color slip. As soon as pieces are hard enough to handle, applique your decorative design on your ash tray or box. This blend of colors in their casting stage makes further color unnecessary. Steps saved in developing an attractive piece frequently make it possible for the hobbyist to compete successfully against the commercial markets, with respect to price-card salability.

Red and white clay which have been wedged separately and then casually mixed together and worked into a form will frequently develop interesting effects when complete, but it is impossible to guarantee duplication of an exact effect, due to the unevenness and irregularity of the manual mixing.

A design is being scratched into this vase and will be brought out with engobe or slip painting. Glaze will then render colors into a unit.

In the color wheel at right, the primary colors, red, blue and yellow, are indicated by the letter A. These are the basic colors used in mixing. Secondary colors, created by blending primary colors, are marked with the letter B. The tertiary colors, made by the mixing of secondary hues with primary colors, are tagged C. Complementary colors are the result of mixing the primary, secondary and tertiary colors. These are shown by connecting lines. The so-called adjacent colors are shown next to each other around the color wheel.

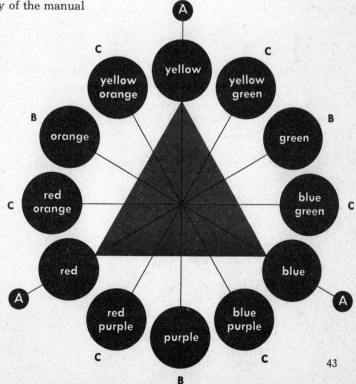

43

How to Make Engobe

Engobe is a method of decoration, since the two clays are of different colors. Any piece of ware may be designed, decorated or colored in full or in part by the use of colored liquid clay or clays.

There are several methods of applying engobe to a piece of ware. The dipping method, faience work, was developed in Florence, Italy, and meant wholly covering one piece of ware with a different colored clay, thereby changing the exterior color of the piece of ware and giving the impression of a solid piece of the texture of the surface. This makes it possible to add a clear glaze and complete the procedure from plastic to finished ware in one operation of firing.

Engobe work permits applying several colors in design and in raised embossed or relief work. Engobe coloring frequently is used to color the inside of ware with one shade and the outside with another. There are also varieties made by adding a colored design and leaving a band of natural basic clay to show them. Then with one application of clear glaze, either gloss or matt, these give the appearance of an interestingly constructed and decorated piece of ware.

Many engobes are naturally colored clay.

Victorian clay will turn to a rich mahogany when fired between cone .02 and .06. But when fired to cone .02 it becomes a rich black.

Dalton No. 93 becomes a brick red when fired, becoming darker as it is fired higher. There are many shades in buff, pink, or white.

Most other colors are artificially made by adding body stain to the clay body in liquid form or by mixing powdered stain into the dry flour and milling, or mixing thoroughly.

In making engobe by this method, it must be applied upon a piece of ware still unfired and in its plastic or leather state. The reason that this homemade engobe in simple form can be used only under these conditions is that dissimilar bodies, unless blended together while moist, will not adhere to each other and the engobe may chip off during firing.

In order to make an engobe which can be used with most clays, it is advisable to start with a finely ground dry clay and calcine (or calcinit). Fire it in your kiln. This process preshrinks or calcines, and changes the nature of the clay. If this body is already colored, such as Dalton No. 93 or other naturally colored clay, it may be mixed with water and a few drops of glaze gum until it has reached the consistency

A ball mill, used to mix clay bodies with engobe stains, can be made from revolving rods and a jar in which carborundum balls or marbles are placed.

Jars of varying size may be used on the ball mill. As the jars rotate, the balls pulverize the mixture. Ordinarily, a complete job may take several hours.

of light cream. If this mixture should not flow off a brush smoothly, a small amount of glycerine may be added for smoother flowing; also a small amount (less than 2% by weight) of clear glaze. This type of engobe may be applied upon most clay bodies in any state—plastic, leather hard, dry, or even bisque.

It should be remembered, however, that the drier the piece of ware, the more fluid should be your engobe, since a dry piece of ware absorbs moisture more rapidly than a moist or leather-hard piece of ware. If your engobe is to be made with artificial colors, choose a good white body finely milled, and place this on a shelf, or the floor of your kiln. This dry mixture may be placed on any kiln shelf and either laid loosely or in a heap. It may be fired rapidly either alone in the kiln or with other ware. It should be fired to any cone between .02 and .06. When the kiln is opened, the pile of clay will appear exactly as it was before firing except that it will have lost some weight. To this calcined body, add 2% to 10% dry body stain. Pastels or lighter shades will require greater concentration of color than darker shades.

This mixture will require thorough mixing to blend the color evenly. The simplest mixer is a ball mill. A ball mill in industrial use is usually a large vat or barrel with the

JAR SPECIFICATIONS

SIZE	Actual Capacity in Quarts	Ball Charge in Pounds	Grinding Capacity in Pounds of 100 lb. Cu. ft. Sand	Approx. Net Shipping Wt.	Approximate Export Wt.
Metal Covered Porcelain Jars					
1 Quart	1¼	2	1	12 lb.	20 lb.
1-Gallon	4¾	10	5	26	33
2 Gallon	11	15	10	53	60
Porcelain Jars—Large Neck					
1 Quart	1	2	1	5	8
1 Gallon	5½	10	5	20	25
2 Gallon	2.7 Gal.	20	10	25	33
4 Gallon	4.4 Gal.	40	15	40	50
6 Gallon	6.8 Gal.	60	25	50	60
Porcelain Jars—Small Neck					
1 Gallon	1	8	4½	10	15
1½ Gallon	1½	———	———	18	23
2 Gallon	2	15	9	23	31
3 Gallon	3	22	13½	27	37
4 Gallon	4	30	18	33	46
5 Gallon	5	38	22½	38	48
6 Gallon	6	46	27	52	63

In operation, the ball mill may hold two or three jars at once. Note that rubber bands have been put around the jars to prevent slippage against rods.

A pulley arrangement and reduction shaft, driven by a fractional hp motor, plus a secondary shaft with two pulleys completes mechanism needed.

opening on one side. The barrel is sealed at both ends. This container is made of very hard material such as porcelain or stainless steel. Into this vat or barrel is poured the material to be mixed and pulverized. Hard balls or marbles of carborundum are then added, and the side opening closed. The barrel is then revolved for several hours. The action of the carborundum balls tumbling over and over crush and mix the material in this drum.

A very simple type ball mill for hobby, home, or studio use is made by setting two parallel rods in sleeves or ball bearing brackets. so that the rods will revolve freely. Mount the supporting brackets so the rods will revolve freely and so that the parallel bars are between 3" and 4" apart. Allow the rods to be 30" and 36" long respectively. When these rods are mounted in their bearing supports, allow one bar to project 6" beyond its bracket. This is for mounting a driven pulley. Place a 6" pulley on this extension of one bar. It is important for the bar to revolve slowly. Therefore, a reduction shaft and pulley arrangement will have to be used to assure slow operation.

Set up a secondary shaft with two pulleys, one pulley 1½" in diameter and one pulley 5" in diameter.

Align the 1½" pulley in line with the large pulley on the end of the first steel rod. Connect these two pulleys with a belt. Set up a standard motor of not less than ⅙ hp. with a 1½" pulley on the motor shaft, and align this pulley with the 5" pulley of the secondary shaft. Join these pulleys with a belt. When your motor revolves now at its normal speed of 1725-1750 rpm, the one longer shaft will revolve at a considerably reduced speed.

A jar, 5" or 6" in diameter resting between the parallel bars will, by the action of the driven bar, revolve itself, and cause the second bar, which is freely suspended, to revolve also.

This will prove a very effective ball mill, or mixer. A can or jar of slip which may have settled, or a mixture of glaze which is out of suspension, will be rapidly restored to its original condition when subjected to the revolving motors of this machine. For grinding or milling add a handful of marbles in a jar and start the motor. The duration of the operation will have a direct bearing on the fineness of the resultant powder and mixing process, and when your material has been thoroughly mixed and milled, open the jar. Remove marbles and your mixture is complete. This machine will be helpful in mixing and preparing engobe.

Colors Imparted by Oxides and Other Substances

Oxide	Formula	Color
Aluminum	Al_2O_3	None
Antimony	Sb_2O_3	None
Barium	BaO	None
Bismuth	Bi_2O_3	Pearl
Boric	B_2O_3	None
Cadmium	CdO	None
Calcium	CaO	None
Cerium	CeO_2	None
Chromium	Cr_2O_3	Green, pink, red
Cobalt	CoO	Blue, violet
Copper	CuO	Red, green, blue
Iridium	IrO_2	Gray
Iron	FeO	Black, green, red, brown
Lead	PbO	None
Magnesium	MgO	None
Manganese	MnO	Brown, purple, pink, black
Nickel	NiO	Brown, yellow, purple, violet, blue
Phosphorus	P_2O_5	None
Potassium	K_2O	None
Silicon	SiO_2	None
Silver	Ag_2O	Gray, yellow
Sodium	Na_2O	None
Strontium	SrO	None
Tin	SnO_2	None
Titanium	TiO_2	None
Uranium	U_3O_8	Yellow, green, ivory
Zinc	ZnO	None
Zirconium	ZrO_2	None

Other Substances

Substance	Formula	Color
Albany slip		Red, brown
Cadmium sulfide	CdS	Yellow
Gold compounds		Red, rose, purple, gold
Lead antimonate		Yellow
Lead chromate		Orange
Platinum		Gray
Selenium		Red, pink, amber
Sulfur		Amber
Zinc		Blue, green

Checked by Harshaw Chemical Co.

Decorating Data

Crushed glass in colors, when fired in a dish or bowl, appears to be colored cracked ice and makes a unique decoration.

Impressing a grid design by pressing a dishrag onto a slab of clay which is going to be used for a basket or dish bottom, offers an eye-appealing change.

Decalcomanias are a popular means of decorating ceramic ware and may be obtained in various patterns.

Decalcomanias

Decalcomanias are designs printed in color specifically prepared for use in decorating ceramic ware by transferring. The designs are applied to bisque ware and rubbed down with stiff, bristled brushes to insure complete adherence.

For decals printed on duplex paper, the following steps are recommended:

1. Strip the thin tissue from the heavy backing paper.

2. Varnish the ware to be decorated with a thin coat of decal varnish which has been diluted with 40% to 50% turpentine.

3. Allow the varnish to become tacky, then apply the decals face-down on the varnish and rub with a slightly moist stiff brush until perfect contact has been made between the decal and the ware.

4. Apply water until the tissue paper floats away. Do not pull the paper off the ware. •

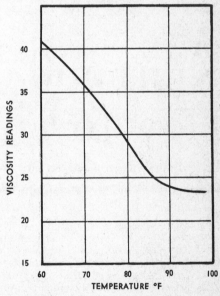

Effect of Temperature on Viscosity of Decal Varnish

VISCOSITY READINGS

40

35

30

25

20

15

60   70   80   90   100

TEMPERATURE °F

A sponge and decal brush are all the tools you require to apply decalcomanias. Follow maker's advice.

Varnishing ware   Applying the decals   Allowing ware to dry

Photos by
Robert Brightman

Kilns and How to Construct Them

Front door type, top loader, square or cylinder—

you pick your materials and you take your choice.

THERE are many types of kilns, or heat treating ovens, in use. Most ceramists use a periodic kiln. This means a kiln which has a complete cycle from cold, to warm, to hot, to cooling, and to cold, as contrasted with larger industrial kilns which maintain constant heat and through which ware is passed on specially designed cars.

A periodic kiln, or oven, is no different in performance from any other type of oven except that it reaches very high temperatures. This heat causes chemical changes in clay and glaze, just as your oven causes changes to take place in food. The construction of a kiln is far simpler than would be the construction of a cookstove. Many different types of fuels for kilns are in use for heating to the required temperatures.

The most suitable means for general use is electricity, since it is extremely flexible and reasonable in most parts of the United States and Canada.

Once the source of power or heat is decided, the next decision is the quantity of this fuel available for the operation of your kiln, since if only normal electricity for lighting is available, then your kiln size or firing area is limited to just that power. For example, a 9″ cube may be heated to 2000 degrees in about five hours, using 110-120 volts at 15 amperes, or 1650 watts, i.e. volts X amperes equal watts. (Watt's law.) Note that Kw (Kilowatt) equals 1000 watts. The foregoing indicates some relationship between heat and watts. It is important to consider "heat loss," since obviously if the

1650 watts were consumed in an open area there would be no appreciable heat rise, but if the same 1650 watts were consumed in a confined area, the rise in temperature would become immediately apparent. Hence, we must conclude that our kiln must be in a confined area, and heavily insulated as well, in order to prevent too great a heat loss. It follows, too, that the more power available, the larger the interior of a kiln may be. The same general pattern for all sizes and shapes may be followed in construction. Once you know what power you may use and relate that to the size of kiln you want, you are ready to acquire the material needed for assembly.

The final consideration is whether to make a front door opening, which is somewhat more complicated, or to make a top-loading kiln. In either event, a suitable container should be obtained for the shell. A 55-gallon drum, cut down to the desired height, would make an ideal container for a square, round, or hexagonal top-loading kiln. Even an old tin breadbox would make a shell for a front-door type kiln, provided the edges were reinforced with angle iron. Best of all for the front-door type kiln would be to construct your own frame of iron, and weld the corners together.

Frame size should be determined by interior area, i.e., a 9" muffle or firing area should have not less than 4½" of insulation on all sides, hence a top-loading kiln should be in a drum or a container at least 18" in diameter and 18" high, or a front-door kiln should be in a shell 18" cubed. A 12" kiln would also require at least 4½"

of insulation on each side, top and bottom. An 18" kiln would require 6" of insulation on each side, top and bottom—and so on proportionately. The larger the firing area, the thicker would be the insulating material required.

For simple rules of construction applying either to the top-loading or front-door kiln, it is necessary to consider your needs and your facilities. For the top-loader, the materials needed are: an oil barrel or other metal shell at least 18" in diameter; one carton of insulating brick (25 bricks 4½"x2½"x9"), the type which can be cut with a saw or knife, for top-loading kiln, or one and one-half cartons of this brick for a front-door kiln. These are carried by all oil burner supply companies or lumber yards. They are made in several qualities, designed to withstand 2000 degrees, or 2300 degrees, or even 2600 degrees without deterioration. The 2000 degrees brick is entirely satisfactory. Also needed: about 125 feet of Nickel Chromium (Nichrome) wire, which has a limit temperature of 2050 degrees Fahrenheit, or Kanthal A1 wire, which has a limit temperature of 2462 degrees Fahrenheit; in the Nichrome wire size .045 B&S measurement No. 17 rated at approximately ⅓ ohm per foot, or, in the ferrous wire (Kanthal) size .045 B&S measurement No. 16 rated at approximately ⅓ ohm per foot is required. The wire should cost at retail not more than $7.00 per 100 feet. Finally, you will also need one tub of high temperature cement (25 lbs.), one double pole, double throw toggle switch, rated at 20 amperes, 125 volts. These should be

A 55 gallon drum, cut down to desired height, will make a suitable container for a top-loading kiln.

Another favorite style of kiln is the front-door loading type, made of sheet metal and angle iron.

Four principal types of switch are used on kilns where electricity is used for heating. All of these are basically similar, except that heavier switches will give you longer service with greater safety.

available through your local electric supply house or mail order house. They are manufactured by Cutler Hammer; Arrow, Hart and Hegeman; Carlin, and so on. The price may vary for this switch. Some are available through war surplus outlets. Then get a two gallon tin or other tin or steel box for electric connections, approximately 10 inches high and 4 to 6 inches wide. This box needs no back. Two asbestos shingles or transite are also needed for a panel; and a few brass nuts and screws for binding posts; three 3" porcelain tubes used in regular knob and tube wiring; approximately ten feet of asbestos-impregnated wire B&S No. 14 for internal wiring; the necessary lead wire and plug to your receptacle, which should be heavy electric iron cord and a heavy duty 15 ampere plug; four 12" threaded rods ¼" diameter with two bolts and washers for each rod; several scraps of tin from the same can which will make your electric box; one dozen sheet metal screws

and a few small nuts and bolts; and one or two bushels of rock wool or mica pellets (vermiculae) for insulation. The tools needed are few in number and are usually found in the average home workshop. They consist of:

Brace and several bits for metal (⅛, ⅜, ½, ¾ inch)
Curtain rod ⅜" by at least 18" long
Old paint brush
Cold chisel ½" cutting edge
Pair needle-nosed pliers with cutter
Grinding wheel ⅜" thick or piece of abrasive ⅜" wide to groove out insulating brick
Screwdriver with about ½" edge
Pair of tin snips.

For the front-door kiln the same equipment is needed except for the oil drum and threaded rods. In place of the oil drum for a shell you will require an angle-iron frame at least ⅜"x¼" either welded at

An easy way to coil heating elements is to use an ordinary curtain rod as a mandrel. With one end of the rod in a brace, secure the other end in hole in wall as a guide. Wire is clamped onto rod and tension exerted in turns.

Bricks, making up sides of the kiln, are grooved half-inch deep to accept the heating wires.

Aligning the grooved bricks for assembly. The grooves are cut out with a chisel and a hammer.

Floor of kiln is bound with wire so that it can be lifted and placed in the bottom of drum as a unit.

The floor of the kiln should be tightly wedged against the sides of the drum with scrap brick.

All touching surfaces of brick are coated with the high temperature cement applied with a stiff brush.

After side walls are cemented and erected in place, they too are wedged in place with scrap brick.

Porcelain tubes are inserted through asbestos shingles, through the drum and into pre-drilled brick.

The two shingles are spaced so that binding posts for current do not touch the metal drum.

A two-gallon can, cut down the center, covers the electrical connections. Cord is No. 14 gauge.

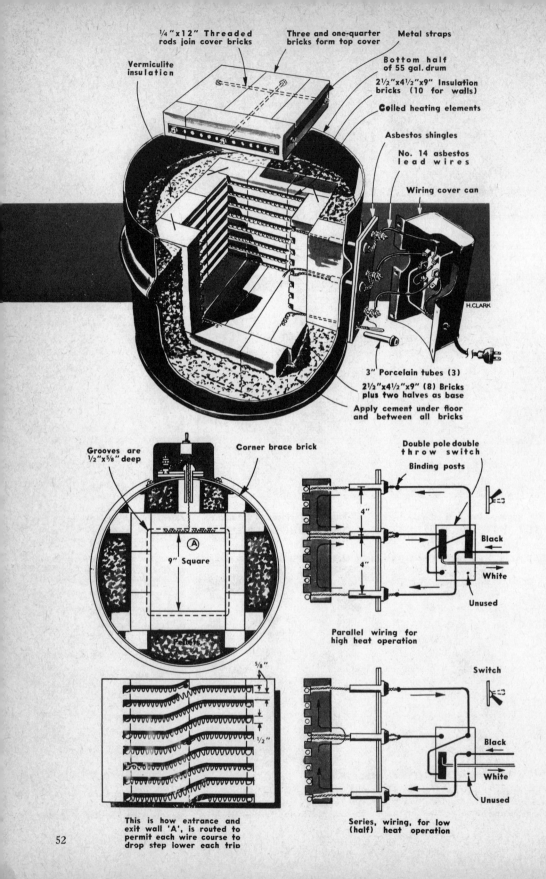

¼"x12" Threaded rods join cover bricks

Three and one-quarter bricks form top cover

Metal straps

Vermiculite insulation

Bottom half of 55 gal. drum

2½"x4½"x9" Insulation bricks (10 for walls)

Coiled heating elements

Asbestos shingles

No. 14 asbestos lead wires

Wiring cover can

H. CLARK

3" Porcelain tubes (3)

2½"x4½"x9" (8) Bricks plus two halves as base

Apply cement under floor and between all bricks

Grooves are ½"x⅝" deep

Corner brace brick

Double pole double throw switch

Binding posts

Ⓐ

9" Square

4"

4"

Black

White

Unused

Parallel wiring for high heat operation

⅝"

½"

Switch

Black

White

Unused

This is how entrance and exit wall 'A', is routed to permit each wire course to drop step lower each trip

Series, wiring, for low (half) heat operation

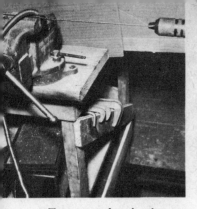

Three strands of wire are twisted as shown to make a lead to the binding posts.

Wire, coiled by wrapping around a ⅜ in. dowel, is now inserted into chiseled grooves.

Next step is to pour Vermiculite, a mineral insulating material, into all open spaces.

The heating elements are pinned in the routes at intervals of two or three inches.

Bricks that form the cover are cemented and held together by threaded rods, metal straps.

The switch box is secured to the steel frame with Parker screws. Kiln is now complete.

corners to form a cube, or drilled to be joined at corners with nuts and bolts; six sheets of tin or metal not thinner than 20 gauge or at least $\frac{3}{16}$″ thickness transite sheets. You will need four to five dozen Parker screws; two extra 18″ lengths of 2″x⅛″x13″ long angle iron which will become the door jamb and frame; also four pieces to form a door frame 12¼″x12¼″— welded to form a square. Also two butts 1½″x3″ and any type door catch, similar to bar slide lock or drop catch. If welding is to be the method you prefer, unless you own welding equipment, it would be best to have your iron shop or blacksmith at least weld the frame, hinges, and door.

Construction Steps

To make a top-loading kiln:
1. Cut barrel or drum to allow a height of 18″.
2. Lay nine insulating blocks together.
3. Use ten bricks for the four sides and route to allow eight rows. Routes are ⅝″ deep and ½″ wide.

4. The top is made of 3¼″ brick laid together. These are drilled with holes made by using the rod in the chuck or brace. Rods are then placed through brick with washer and bolts and scrap tin.

Once your brick and container are set up, dismantle and start the actual construction by thinning out high temperature cement with water to the consistency of cream. Paint bottom of barrel with a coat of cement and paint the bottom side or sides of each-brick with the same mixture of cement. Place brick in position as in step two, exerting pressure to squeeze brick against cement. Erect sides, brushing a generous amount of cement on each touching surface. Insert wedges between brick and barrel inside to keep brick from slipping out of position. Wedges may be made of scraps of brick or even common field stone. They are used only to reinforce the sides of the kiln. It is important to be sure you have plenty of high temperature bricks, which will form your top core.

5. Take fifty feet of resistance wire ⅓ ohm per foot and bend double one foot at

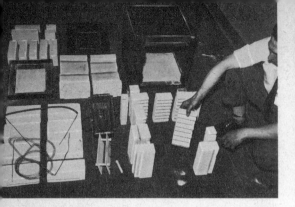

Complete layout of material is shown for the simple construction of a top-loading ceramic kiln.

When completely assembled, kiln will look like this, ready to be stacked with ware and fired.

the end, clamping this point of wire to a curtain rod or other pole which is to be used as your mandril. This rod should be ⅜" in diameter. Secure your rod in the chuck of a brace and put the other end of the rod in any convenient hole as a guide. Turn brace so that your resistance wire winds into a tight coil. Wind until only two feet of wire is left unwound and treat this as the beginning lead was treated. Twist the leads at both ends. Repeat with the next fifty feet of resistance wire.

6. Measure length of four rows of routes in your brick kiln and stretch your coil to this length. Embed coil in these rows and repeat for the second set of four rows.

7. From an asbestos shingle or piece of transite, bakelite, or other insulating material, cut two pieces for electric panel 10" high x 4" wide. Drill three ½" holes for porcelain tubes through both pieces of transite and through drum or shell and through brick into bottom, top, and center groove. These holes are drilled so that their centers are 1" in from the left edge. The top hole is 1" from the top edge. The bottom hole is 1" from the bottom edge. Center hole is approximately 4" above bottom hole and 4" below top hole. Opposite these holes drill 1" in from right edge, and, through only one thickness of transite, three holes for binding posts. These are to be the diameter of the screws you obtained for that purpose. By drilling through only one thickness and inserting your screw and nuts, the second thickness, which is pierced only by the porcelain tubes, insulates the head of the screw from the metal shell. Drill two small holes for Parker screws to secure transite panel lightly to the steel shell.

8. From the remaining wire cut 2" lengths and bend in the shape of a hairpin with needle-nosed pliers. Force the pins into the brick grooves every few inches

to keep the coils from crawling out of position.

9. Cut a two gallon oil can vertically through the center and flange the edge. This will become your switch holder and electric box. It is held in place by Parker screws. Mount your switch on the side. Make all connections through binding posts, using asbestos-impregnated wire, No. 14 or heavier, and using for your service line asbestos—insulated stranded iron cord and your heavy duty plug. Be sure to employ a 25 or 30 ampere fuse in your fuse box if there are other circuits on the same line, since the kiln draws 15 amperes.

For the front-door kiln either weld or bolt angle iron to form a rigid cube. This iron frame for the door should have hinges welded or bolted to frame of the kiln. These hinges should be the removable pin type to allow for separation of the butt parts so that the door may be worked separately. Metal sheets of 18 or 20 gauge are cut and either welded or secured with Parker screws or nuts and bolts to hold sheet metal to sides, bottom, rear, and door front. It is advisable to leave top off until complete. Floor is formed by laying eight bricks together. Nine bricks are needed for the sides. Routes are made under the top-loader. Note, however, that only three sides contain coils. The top is constructed by placing six full bricks and two half bricks together. Eight bricks set in the door frame are tightly wedged. All bricks are secured together in the same manner described in step 4 earlier. The door packed solid with brick must now be trimmed to fit the opening of the kiln. This is best done by using a wood saw to cut the door to approximately the size of the opening, and then hanging the door by the hinges and filing or making use of other abrasives to shave the door projection to fit the opening of the kiln or muffle. All other steps are identical

Representative Refractory Shapes

9" STRAIGHT
9" x 4½" x 2½"
FIRECLAY, SILICA, BASIC

SMALL 9"
9" x 3½" x 2½"
FIRECLAY, SILICA, BASIC

9" SOAP
9" x 2¼" x 2½"
FIRECLAY, SILICA, BASIC

9" No. 1 SPLIT
9" x 4½" x 1¼"
FIRECLAY, SILICA, BASIC

9" No. 3 ARCH
9" x 4½" x (2½"—1")
FIRECLAY, SILICA, BASIC

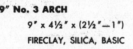

9" No. 1-X WEDGE
9" x 4½" x (2½"—2¼")
FIRECLAY, SILICA, BASIC

9" CIRCLE BRICK
(9"—A) x 4½" x 2½"
FIRECLAY

9" 48° END SKEW
(9"—6¾") x 4½" x 2½"
FIRECLAY, SILICA, BASIC

9" 48° SIDE SKEW
9" x (4½"—2¼") x 2½"
FIRECLAY, SILICA, BASIC

9" 60° END SKEW
(9"—7⅚") x 4½" x 2½"
FIRECLAY, SILICA

9" 60° SIDE SKEW
9" x (4½"—3⅟₁₆") x 2½"
FIRECLAY, SILICA, BASIC

9" EDGE SKEW
9" x (4½"—1½") x 2½"
FIRECLAY, SILICA, BASIC

9" No. 4 KEY
9" x (4½"—2¼") x 2½"
FIRECLAY, SILICA, BASIC

9" FEATHER EDGE
9" x 4½" x (2½"—⅛")
FIRECLAY, SILICA, BASIC

9" JAMB
9" x 4½" x 2½"
FIRECLAY, SILICA, BASIC

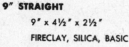

9" NECK
9" x 4½" x (2½"—⅝")
FIRECLAY, SILICA, BASIC

to the round kiln. Be sure to fill all openings between the sides and the shell with insulation material, as well as covering the top with "vermiculae" before placing the sheet metal cover on top. Painting with aluminum paint will give your kiln the appearance of a factory-produced oven. Your final step is to secure the catch on the door and the frame; this will hold the door tightly shut while operating the kiln.

In both the top-loading and front-door kilns a peephole should be cut into either the door or the side in order that you may observe the cone or color. A ½" bit will cut a suitable hole. Exercise care not to cut into a coil on the top-loader. Front-door kilns may have a hole in the door. Make a plug to fit the hole from scrap brick so that the peephole is closed at all times, except during observation. •

By John B. Kenny

Make This Hexagonal Kiln

UNTIL recently pottery kilns were quite expensive and building your own was a difficult operation. Two new developments in the ceramic field, however, have reduced considerably the expense and the effort. One of these is a new kind of brick which combines both refractory and insulating properties. The other is a wire called Kanthal which can be used for electric elements and withstands higher temperatures than any wire elements previously known.

A word or two about the bricks. The problem in kiln construction is to provide generating heat—and keeping it confined. Formerly the only bricks that could be used on the inside portions of kilns were refractory bricks. These are heavy and extremely dense. They can stand high temperatures all right but they also conduct heat readily. A kiln built of such bricks alone would lose most of its heat right through the walls. When they are used for a kiln lining it is necessary to put a layer of insulating material like bloated mica or glass fiber around them and then build another layer of insulating brick on the outside. Ordinary insulating bricks are soft, porous and will not readily conduct heat. But they cannot stand high temperatures. One of these used on the inside of a kiln would crumble during firing. The new bricks, on the other hand, are porous and do not conduct heat readily, yet they can stand high temperatures. I have seen one end of such a brick held in a flame until it became red hot. The other end was still cool enough to hold in my hand.

Insulating refractory brick can be bought directly from manufacturers of refractories or from ceramic supply houses. They come in different grades, numbered 20, 22, 26, etc. The number indicates the temperature the brick will stand. No. 20 is good for 2000° F,

Make your basic hexagonal pattern on cardboard by setting compass at 8½ in. and scribing circle. Divide the circumference into six equal parts.

For the first layer of the kiln floor, align the bricks along the edges of your hexagon and mark off with soft pencil all the ends that will have to be cut.

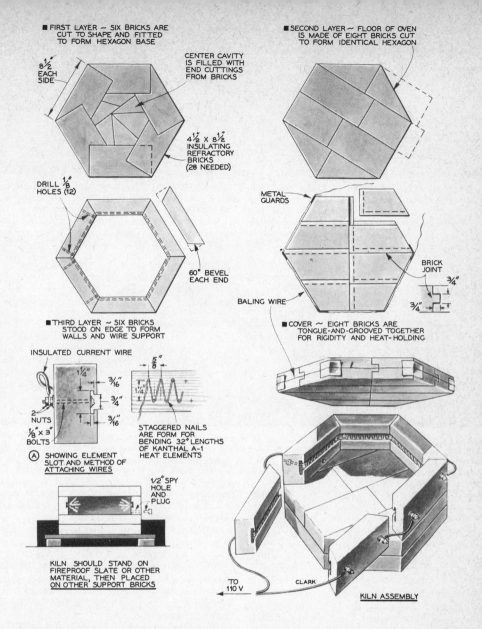

■ FIRST LAYER ~ SIX BRICKS ARE CUT TO SHAPE AND FITTED TO FORM HEXAGON BASE

8½ EACH SIDE

CENTER CAVITY IS FILLED WITH END CUTTINGS FROM BRICKS

4½ x 8½ INSULATING REFRACTORY BRICKS (28 NEEDED)

DRILL ⅛" HOLES (12)

60° BEVEL EACH END

■ THIRD LAYER ~ SIX BRICKS STOOD ON EDGE TO FORM WALLS AND WIRE SUPPORT

INSULATED CURRENT WIRE

1¼"
3/16"
3/4"
3/16"

2 NUTS
⅛" x 3" BOLTS

5/8"
1¼"

STAGGERED NAILS ARE FORM FOR BENDING 32" LENGTHS OF KANTHAL A-1 HEAT ELEMENTS

Ⓐ SHOWING ELEMENT SLOT AND METHOD OF ATTACHING WIRES

½" SPY HOLE AND PLUG

KILN SHOULD STAND ON FIREPROOF SLATE OR OTHER MATERIAL, THEN PLACED ON OTHER SUPPORT BRICKS

■ SECOND LAYER ~ FLOOR OF OVEN IS MADE OF EIGHT BRICKS CUT TO FORM IDENTICAL HEXAGON

METAL GUARDS

BRICK JOINT
¾"
¾"

BALING WIRE

■ COVER ~ EIGHT BRICKS ARE TONGUE-AND-GROOVED TOGETHER FOR RIGIDITY AND HEAT-HOLDING

TO 110 V

CLARK

KILN ASSEMBLY

A hand saw, specifically a back saw, is the best tool for making these cuts. Do not discard the scraps—they will complete the kiln's first layer.

The channel for the electrical element may be dug out with a chisel, but this accessory tool will save lots of time. (See text for details.)

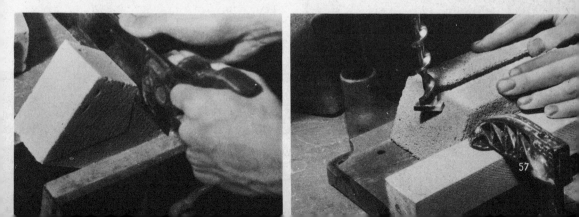

57

 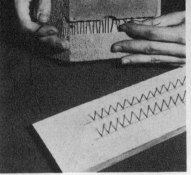 

To facilitate getting electrical element to proper shape, nail some brads to a piece of scrap and bend wire around them as shown.

Bricks are wired individually. One of the two ⅛-in. holes for the binding posts is visible at left. Note angle of brick end.

Assembled kiln without the top. Use No. 14 single-strand wire to connect binding posts. Two wires at right lead to male plug.

Tongue-and-groove all joints of the kiln top, employing the same technique used in making the notches for electrical element.

Cut the tongues about ¾ in. high. For maximum heat conservation use this type of joint on the brick ends as well as the sides.

Rub bricks together to assure a good, snug fit. You will need eight properly cut bricks in all to complete the lid of the kiln.

No. 22 will go to 2200°, and so on. For the kiln we are going to build, No. 22 or 26 will do. We shall need a total of 26 bricks.

Kanthal wire or ribbon is made of an alloy recently developed in Sweden. It can stand temperatures up to 2460°—hot enough to fire stoneware or even low-temperature porcelain.

A number of potters have built small hexagonal kilns, using the bricks described above, and have wired them with Kanthal elements. Such kilns are inexpensive, easy to make and quite satisfactory in operation. Here is how the job is done.

Start by drawing a hexagon with sides 8½ in. long (the length of a brick). To do this set a compass for a radius of 8½ in. and draw a circle. With the compass at the same setting, divide the circumference of the circle into six equal parts. Connect the dividing points with straight lines and you have a hexagon.

The floor of the kiln is made of two layers of refractory insulating brick lying flat. The first layer will be made of six bricks cut to the shape shown and then put together to form a hexagon.

A simple way to plan the cutting is shown in the photographs. The bricks are laid on

Sheet metal guards prevent the baling wire from cutting into the bricks. For safety's sake, stand the kiln on some fireproof material when it's in use.

the hexagon pattern so that they form alternate sides, then another brick is placed on top of the other two in such a way that it forms the intervening side. The portion where the top brick overlaps those underneath is then marked with a pencil. The marked brick is placed in a vise and the designated portion is sawed out with a back saw.

These bricks can be cut with a hand saw. When six bricks are cut, they are fitted together to make a hexagon. The pieces cut off the ends can be used to fill up the center opening and will make a complete layer. Construct the second layer as indicated.

The walls of the kiln are made of six bricks stood on edge, with the corners mitred at 60° angles so that when they are placed together they form a perfect hexagon. It is necessary to cut a slot for the element in each brick. This can be made by clamping the brick in a vise and making two straight cuts along the center with a back saw. The cuts should be ¾ in. apart and ½ in. deep. The portion between the cuts is then gouged out with a chisel. The channel cut this way can then be widened at the base with a rasp. If you have access to a milling machine, a better way to cut this slot is with a milling cutter. At the University of New Hampshire Experimental Station, where a number of electric kilns have been built, a simple tool was devised for this purpose by grinding the point off a ¾-in. wood bit and brazing a piece of steel $\frac{3}{16}$ in. thick, ½ in. wide, and 1¼ in. long to the bottom. This special tool can be placed in a drill press and rotated while bricks are pushed against it. A block clamped to the table guides the bricks under the rotating bit.

The elements for this kiln are made of six pieces of Kanthal A-1 ribbon, 2 ft., 8 in. long bent into zigzag shape and slid into the brick slots. Kanthal will bend when it is new but once it has been heated, it becomes extremely brittle and no change can be made in its shape. It would be possible to make the element for this kiln out of one piece of wire 16 ft. long, but it is easier to wire each brick separately. When bent to shape the ribbon is inserted in the brick slot. Two holes ⅛ in. in diameter are bored through each brick at the ends of the slot and two ⅛x3-in. bolts are used as binding posts. Thus each brick with its element becomes a separate unit. The units are connected with loops of wire on the outside of the kiln.

Next the roof. For extra strength and to prevent loss of heat through cracks, the bricks forming the roof are put together with tongue and groove joints. The grooves are formed by making straight cuts with a back saw and then gouging out the portion between with a chisel. The tongues are also cut with the saw.

The roof must be lifted off and on, so baling wire is used to tie the bricks together. Metal guards cut from tin cans are placed at the corners to keep the wire from cutting into the bricks. This makes the roof a strong unit which can be easily moved. The bricks forming the wall can be wired together in similar fashion and so can each of the two layers of the base, but it is not necessary—the kiln will work just as well if the wall and the base sections are merely placed tightly together.

Bore a hole ½ in. in diameter through one of the wall bricks. This serves as a spy hole through which you can watch the cones during the kiln firing. A plug for the spy hole is whittled out of one of the brick scraps.

The photo at the bottom of page 58 shows the completed kiln ready for firing. It has inner walls 6 in. on each side and 4½ in. high and contains about 420 cubic inches. There are certain advantages to this shape since it is well suited to most pottery forms, and the fact that the elements go around all sides enables even distribution of heat.

This kiln can be plugged into a 110-volt circuit fused for 25 amperes, but there should be no other electrical equipment on the line. It can reach a temperature of 2000° in about six hours.

Two words of caution. Even though the floor is made of two layers of brick there will be a lot of heat seeping through. The kiln should stand on some fireproof material such as a slab of slate. For additional safety the slab should also be supported on bricks.

The second word of caution concerns the elements. As we said before, Kanthal becomes extremely brittle after it has been heated. Therefore see that the elements are securely fastened to the binding posts and that the binding posts are securely fastened to the bricks. Any movement here is liable to break the element. •

Careful assembly of refractory bricks is vital. A close fit insures maximum heat confinement.

Sculpted pieces, when hollow, should be stuffed
with newspaper or have an armature inside which
will burn out in firing, distributing heat well.

Preparing for Bisque Firing

**You may fire when you are ready, but trust in
kiln furniture and keep your ceramic ware dry.**

ALL ware must be bone dry before firing. If attention is not paid to this paramount rule, disaster will result in that all your effort may be undone.

Because of the thickness of the clay, the surface moisture will be extracted first and the piece will appear dry. However, it will feel cold to the touch. If fired at this time, the moisture within the clay becomes steam which will expand with terrific pressure and crack or explode your ware. Hence, the important rule is to make sure your ware is bone dry.

Among the general preparations required for using your kiln, are, first, the necessity for kiln furniture—stilts, shelves, or set-ters. These terms are best understood if you consider your kiln as a cupboard with removable shelves, or shelves which rest upon supports of different sizes which, when changed from one size to another, permit raising, lowering, or increasing the number of shelves which can be placed in the area. Such furniture for your kiln is made of heat resistant material. The term "heat resistant" means material which, when exposed to heat, will not crack, split, or melt. This definition applies to all such furniture or supports as you may use from time to time in your kiln. To start with, the minimum requirement to use your kiln to advantage would be two shelves and 12 posts. You can make the posts yourself.

Shelves should be 1" smaller than the kiln floor area. That allows ½" for thermal circulation on all sides, throughout the kiln. A dozen posts should consist of four posts in each of three different sizes. These are ¾"x¾"x3", ¾"x¾"x4", and 1"x1"x5", excellent sizes to start with. The posts may be cut from the same insulating brick used in making your kiln. They are easily cut with a saw or serrated knife. Thirty stilts in assorted sizes are used to support glazed ware off the shelf floor of the kiln.

The bottom of your kiln is always cooler than the top due to thermal flow. This is best understood by realizing that hotter air or water is lighter than cooler samples of the same fluids; hence, the hottest air or water floats to the top of an enclosed box or vessel and the cooler air or liquid drops to the bottom. Reinforced with this knowledge, you should stack your bisque ware to allow the thicker or heavier ware, which cannot endure the rapid temperature change as can thinner ware, to be placed on the bottom or cooler area of the kiln. The thinner or lighter ware, which can tolerate thermal shock, may safely be placed in the upper area of your kiln.

Green or unfired ware pieces may touch one another but not the elements. Green ware may also rest on a clean shelf or on

Posts for supporting shelves in the kiln should be made of refractory brick. This material is easily cut to size with a small saw or a serrated knife.

the floor of the kiln with benefit of stilts. Green ware need not stand; it may lie on its side. Smaller pieces may rest on or in larger pieces. Covers of boxes should be fired while in place on the box.

Sculpted pieces should be stacked separately since there is a greater tendency for such a piece to chip or break in the kiln and thereby destroy other ware. A sculpted piece should be allowed to dry slowly for at least a month. It should be hollow or should have an armature inside which can burn out, leaving the piece hollow. This permits more even distribution of heat through the body of the ware.

Examine sculpted ware thoroughly before firing, since any defects will be exaggerated in the kiln if not improved.

Hand molded or cast pieces are usually thick, too. Therefore, stack as near the bottom of your kiln as possible. Make sure all foreign matter from fettling tools is removed before stacking. If a piece of ware should be solid, carve out an opening to hollow the solid body before firing.

Poured or slip cast pieces are thoroughly dry within a week. Such ware may be placed on the top shelf or in the hottest area of the kiln. It is best not to put a heavy piece within a thin piece as the pressure of weight under heat will frequently destroy the thin piece. The only exception is where two pieces are to fit, such as a box and lid or a sugar bowl and lid. In this case always fire the pieces together in their proper po-sitions. They will not adhere. Make sure, however, that there is a slight allowance for contraction and shrinkage, as the two parts may not shrink proportionately.

The important rule is careful drying. Do not attempt any artificial drying except by infra-red lamp. Most methods of artificial drying tend to dry out surface moisture and allow the inside moisture to remain. This creates the false impression which leads to firing a piece not properly dry with its resultant disappointment.

The purpose of the shelves and posts to support shelves at different levels or heights in the kiln is to avoid the excessive weight on the bottom pieces which would result from stacking one piece upon another until the kiln was full. This latter method would cause the bottom to be subjected to too great a strain during the bisque firing and the normal shrinkage would cause shifting within the kiln while exposed to heat. Such conditions often lead to a complete kiln load's being burned, or at least being deformed.

These simple rules will result in the establishment of proper habits in preparation for successful firing. These rules apply whether you fire professionally or as a hobbyist.

The writer is aware of the temptation of haste, but firing is an art requiring the exertion of patience and care. This type of self-control will benefit both the ceramist and the ware. •

Thicker and heavier ware should be placed on the
bottom of the kiln, which is cooler than the top.
Smaller pieces may be placed inside larger ones.

Thinner or lighter ware, which can withstand the
rapid temperature changes inside the kiln, should
be placed in the upper areas on a supported shelf.

Operating the Kiln

Mastering the firing process is the true test of ceramic skills.

LIKE recipes followed carefully by a cook, clay mixtures and glazes will develop best when used and treated as recommended by the manufacturer of the ingredient. One of the most important and frequent questions is: at what temperature does my clay mature? Or, at what temperature does my glaze mature? At what temperature will my ware dunt, vitrify, or melt? It is important to know by temperature, or otherwise how would you know when to slow down or speed up or shut off the kiln?

Time or duration of fire varies due to weather conditions, weight of ware in the kiln, or mass. Hence, while the time factor is of some importance, it is not sufficiently accurate. A thermometer could not help, since at kiln temperatures most thermometer liquids boil and the container for such a liquid would surely melt. This situation resulted in the use of an old principle— that which states that certain dissimilar metals, when twisted together at the end and welded will, if subjected to heat, develop a minute amount of electricity. The ratio of electricity increases with the intensity of the heat. Several such metals of extreme durability against heat are used for this purpose, and are called thermocouples, among them chromel and alumel, platinum and rhodium, etc. These metals, or thermocouples as we shall properly term them, will tolerate the normal kiln heat. The amount of electricity generated by heat exerted upon the thermocouple tip where needed can be recorded upon a micro-voltmeter.

If a temperature chart or dial is substituted for the calibrated dial or chart from the micro-voltmeter we translate our mircrovolts from electrical energy to heat. This type of device is called a pyrometer, and is universally used as an indicating device to show temperatures in excess of those which can be recorded on everyday thermometers. Pyrometers vary in price, depending upon their accuracy. For the average clay work, a tolerance of 2½% plus or minus is not too far off.

Another method of determining temperature is the use of cones or pellets. Cones are small pieces of clay that melt at a predetermined temperature. They are shaped like pyramids. Each cone bears a number. Pellets are more accurate than cones. The tolerance of a cone is approximately 2% plus or minus, but that of a pellet is less than 1% plus or minus. Peepholes in kilns are really observation posts through which a cone or pellet may be observed. Usually a cone or pellet is placed in a wad of dried clay formed to hold the cone or pellet. This is then placed where it can be observed through the peep-hole. When the cone begins to bend, or the pellet has melted, the temperature, denoted by the number of the cone or pellet, has been reached and the kiln is shut off. These previous methods are manual and require attendance of a kiln operator to observe at short intervals as the time for normal maturity is approaching. The manual operation consists of observation and cutting off power, but as with a watched pot, time seems to move slowly.

Pyrometric cones placed inside a kiln and designed to melt at a predetermined temperature offer usual way of knowing when such heat is achieved.

A peephole in the side of the kiln enables ceramist to observe cones. The critical cone is flanked on each side by higher and lower melting cones.

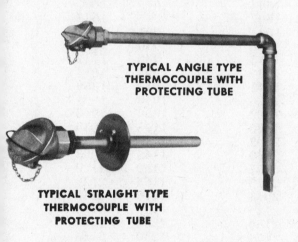

TYPICAL ANGLE TYPE THERMOCOUPLE WITH PROTECTING TUBE

TYPICAL STRAIGHT TYPE THERMOCOUPLE WITH PROTECTING TUBE

Thermocouples, being made of dissimilar metals, are a means of recording temperatures. They tolerate a kiln's heat and register it electrically.

Cones are inclined from the vertical so they bend in the proper direction. A touching position shows ware is mature. This cone was overheated.

COLOR	Degrees Centigrade	Approx. Cone Range	Degrees Fahrenheit
Lowest visible red	475	None	885
Lowest visible red to dark red	475–650	022 – 019	885 – 1200
Dark red to cherry red	650–750	018 – 016	1200 – 1380
Cherry red to bright cherry red	750–815	015 – 014	1380 – 1500
Bright cherry red to orange	815–900	013 – 010	1500 – 1650
Orange to yellow	900–1090	09 – 03	1650 – 2000
Yellow to light yellow	1090–1315	02 – 12	2000 – 2400
Light yellow to white	1315–1540	13 – 20	2400 – 2800
White to dazzling white	1540 and higher	20 and above	2800 and higher

Color Scale for Temperatures (table title)

TEMPERATURE EQUIVALENTS OF PYROMETRIC CONES

Cone Number	Degrees when fired slowly 20 degrees C. per Hr.		Degrees when fired rapidly 150 degrees C. per Hr.	
	Cent.	Fahr.	Cent.	Fahr.
022	585	1085	605	1121
021	595	1103	615	1139
020	625	1157	650	1202
019	630	1166	660	1220
018	670	1238	720	1328
017	720	1328	770	1418
016	735	1355	795	1463
015	770	1418	805	1481
014	795	1463	830	1526
013	825	1517	860	1580
012	840	1544	875	1607
011	875	1607	895	1643
010	890	1634	905	1661
09	930	1706	930	1706
08	945	1733	950	1742
07	975	1787	990	1814
06	1005	1841	1015	1859
05	1030	1886	1040	1904
04	1050	1922	1060	1940
03	1080	1976	1115	2039
02	1095	2003	1125	2057
01	1110	2030	1145	2093
1	1125	2057	1160	2120
2	1135	2075	1165	2129
3	1145	2093	1170	2138
4	1165	2129	1190	2174
5	1180	2156	1205	2201
6	1190	2174	1230	2246
7	1210	2210	1250	2282
8	1225	2237	1260	2300
9	1250	2282	1285	2345
10	1260	2300	1305	2381
11	1285	2345	1325	2417
12	1310	2390	1335	2435
13	1350	2462	1350	2462
14	1390	2534	1400	2552
15	1410	2570	1435	2615
16	1450	2642	1465	2669
17	1465	2669	1475	2687
18	1485	2705	1490	2714
19	1515	2759	1520	2768
20	1520	2768	1530	2786

Because of automatic devices industry and hobbyists needed, there have been developed several automatic devices for cutting off operation of the kiln when the predetermined temperature is achieved. Among the simplest and least expensive is the Kiln-gard. This device consists of two projecting fingers which are introduced into the kiln through the peep-hole. The rear of these arms are spring loaded (outside of the kiln). The spring action exerts a tendency to draw the fingers together. A cone or pellet is placed between the fingers, which extend into the kiln. This keeps the fingers somewhat apart. When the cone or pellet melts, the spring outside the kiln draws the fingers together, since the melting pellet or cone is no longer solid enough to keep them apart.

The fingers also operate a microswitch which is thrown on contact when the fingers of the Kiln-gard are apart and off when the fingers are drawn together. Such a simple device is patented and available all over the United States and Canada.

This device is extremely simple and economical. It will operate efficiently for years, if you follow the instructions attached to the instrument and use a little common sense.

There are other devices available which work on mechanical or electrical impulse, as well as devices which operate on electronic vacuum tubes and intricate circuits.

Weston makes a small device which is activated by the minute electrical flow developed by the heat of the kiln. This power operates a miniature relay to operate a switch for either holding or limiting power based upon the presetting of the control. The Weston Sensitrol and Microrelay, as this device is known, is well accepted in the industrial and commercial field. This writer has observed other limiting or holding devices for kiln operation. Among these are those manufactured by Leeds and Northrup, Hoskins Brown Instrument Company, Minneapolis Honeywell, and Wheelco Instrument Company.

These companies maintain service staffs and consultants in most large cities in the United States, particularly near or in industrial areas, since the controls are widely used in industry. Their costs are high, but their function is extremely accurate. These instruments are to be found in industrial and technical use. Many schools offering courses in ceramics, such as an art or trade schools employ these electronic devices. Each of these instruments also contains, as an integral part of the unit, an indicating pyrometer, which is helpful in disclosing the rate of temperature rise. There has

The "Kiln-gard" is a simple device which automatically shuts off the kiln at the proper temperature.

The arms of the Kiln-gard hold a cone and are put through the kiln's peephole. Then switch is flicked.

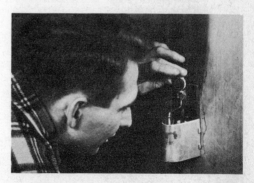

The arms are spring loaded and when the cone melts they touch, activating a turn-off switch.

Indicating Pyrometer (Flush Mounting)

Indicating Pyrometer (Flush or Surface Mounting)

High Resistance Portable Pyrometer

High Resistance Portable Pyrometer

Indicating Resistance Thermometer

Indicating Portable Potentiometer

Simple Pyrometer for Hobby Use

"Sensitrol" Relay and Thermocouple

Volt-Ohm Milliameter

recently been introduced into the retail market a time clock similar to those that turn lights on and off in display windows. This function is based upon a predetermined knowledge of the time the sun sets and artificial lighting should be employed to advantage. Also at a predetermined time, the clock, by preset internal switch, disconnects power for lights. This type of device would be excellent if we could always predetermine firing time or duration. There are many factors to consider here. For example, ware will fire faster during dry weather than during damp, humid weather.

BTU or units of heat which are introduced into a kiln, regardless of fuel, are seldom constant. During the late night hours, more and steadier power is available through your source of electricity than may be available during the day, when industry draws heavily upon the same source. In heating ware in a kiln, each piece requires so many heat units (BTU) to heat it to the maturity temperature. Hence, it follows that a fully loaded kiln will take longer, even if the source of power is constant, than will a partially loaded kiln. A clock device could be set to approximate the time required and by signal device notify the kiln operator that maturity time was approaching. Then the operator could make observations of the cone or pyrometer at five minute intervals.

Most electric kilns available to the hobbyist ready-built are complete with the required instruments. A representative selection of these kilns is pictured in the Equipment Review section.

At left is a selection of devices and instruments the ceramist will find of use in operating kilns.

Semi-Vitreous—Cone 04

Ball clay	40%
Talc	40
Frit	10-20
Flint	0-10

Semi-Vitreous—Cone 04

Nepheline syenite	60%
Ball clay	15
China clay	20
Flint	5

Semi-Vitreous—Cone 1
(All-American Body)

China clay	32%
Tennessee No. 5 ball clay	28
Vitrox	6
Nepheline syenite	6
Talc	6
Dolomite	2
Flint	20

Semi-Vitreous—Cone 1
(All-American Body)

Tennessee ball (Victoria)	21%
Georgia kaolin (Homer)	15
Potash feldspar	40
Flint	19
Talc	5

Casting Body—Cone 06-04

Cardinal Kaolin	200
Robin Ball Clay	200
Nepheline Syenite	432
Cryolite	18
Ferro Frit 3195	150

Casting Body—Cone 6-7

Cardinal Kaolin	250
Robin Ball Clay	250
Potash Feldspar	200
Flint	300

Casting Body—Cone 12
(Vitreous)

Cardinal Kaolin	240
Robin Ball Clay	210
Potash Feldspar	180
Whiting	20
Flint	350

Semi-Vitreous—Cone 3
(All-American Body)

Feldspar	25%
Flint	21
Klondyke washed clay	25
Old Mine No. 4 ball clay	25
Talc	4

Semi-Vitreous—Cone 10
(All-American Body)

Feldspar	17%
Flint	32
Klondyke crude clay	31
Old Mine No. 4 ball clay	20

Vitreous—Cone 10
(All-American Body)

Feldspar	30%
Flint	20
Klondyke washed clay	30
Old Mine No. 4 ball clay	20

Art Ware—Cone 11-12
(All-American Body)

Kamec kaolin	30%
EPK Florida kaolin	7
Old Mine No. 4 ball clay	8
Georgia whiting	2
Flint	35
Feldspar	18

Semi-Vitreous—Cone 04

Imperial Ball Clay	15.0%
Rex Ball Clay	15.0
Monarch China Clay	6.0
Talc	46.0
Nephline Syenite	5.0
Flint	13.0

Talc Type Body
Cone 06-04

C & C	23%
Bandy Black	10
Plastic Vitrox	17
Talc	50

Talc Type Body—Cone 8

Pioneer Kaolin	18.0%
Flint	37.5
Spar	12.0
C & C	17.0
Old Whittier	5.0
Bandy Black	8.0
Whiting	2.5

A representative group of recipes for the making of clay bodies for artware, with cone equivalents.

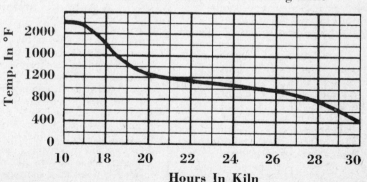

A Desirable Kiln Curve Cooling Zone

Temp. In °F — 2000, 1000, 1200, 800, 400, 0

Hours In Kiln — 10 18 20 22 24 26 28 30

While firing is in progress, do not open the kiln door. Besides damaging ware, the operator may be burned.

Operation of a Kiln for Bisque Firing

Another question that recurs is "What about the cost of operating a kiln? Isn't it expensive to use electricity to heat to such a high temperature? What about upkeep on a kiln?"

Electricity is probably the cheapest commodity in the United States and Canada. A small kiln draws 15 amperes at 115 volts or 1650 watts, or 1.65 kilowatts. Your power is charged on a wattmeter, and you are charged on a kilowatt rate (1000 watts equals 1 kilowatt) per hour. If your local rate is 2c per KWH (kilowatt hour), it would cost you 3.3c per hour to fire. Should your rate be 5c per KWH, it would cost 8¼c an hour to fire. These costs are nominal. Should you possess a large electric kiln and your service be adequate or additional power lines brought to your location, the rates decline sharply, based upon over-all quantity consumed. This rule also applies to gas as a fuel.

In operating your kiln for bisque firing it is necessary to understand what changes are taking place during the firing process in order to operate your kiln to the utmost advantage for your ware. During the heat-

---

A Note of Caution

Never open the kiln door once it is closed and the kiln is fired, until all trace of color has disappeared. Besides the effect of thermal shock on your ware or glaze, there is danger to the operator who places himself in the path of a flow of superheated air. A fire, too, may be started when such heat is released. A fourth danger is the possibility of rupture to your kiln door, as thermal expansion usually makes it fit snugly in its frame and forcing it open may damage it.

ing process certain chemical changes are taking place within your clay body. Heat is releasing chemical moisture from within the body of your clay even though it was apparently "bone dry" before firing. This chemical water is technically known as "water smoke." Once it has been eliminated from your clay, the clay itself has lost for all time its ability to become plastic. It can never again be moistened and wedged into a pliable plastic mass.

It is good practice to start your firing slowly to allow the water smoke to escape slowly and, if possible, allow the door to remain slightly ajar for an hour or two. This permits free escape of this chemical moisture. Even after you close the door of the kiln, leave the peep-hole open until the inside of the kiln begins to develop a red glow from heat. The open peep-hole will act as a vent port for water smoke. You may even notice beads of moisture deposited around the peep-hole and the top portion of your door—an indication of the path of escape.

Once the kiln shows color within, seal it tightly. Firing may then become more rapid by introducing more fuel if the maximum has not already been applied. At the maturity point of your ware (when the cone you have chosen begins to bend) shut off the power of the source of heat. Do not

open either peep-hole or door. Allow the kiln to cool slowly. It is best not to open any portion of the kiln until twice the firing time has elapsed. Then open the door slightly and open the peep-hole. After an hour, open the door one quarter and after another hour you may open the door wide and remove the ware. In all probability, ware will still be too hot to handle with the bare hand. In this event use heavy gloves and do not keep the piece in hand longer than necessary to deposit it upon a piece of transite or insulating material. Hot ware

Keep firing equipment clean. Dust out kilns and wash them. Use a sponge to clean clay off a bat.

In removing fired ware from kiln, use tongs and gloves. Always heat the gripper portion of tongs.

Kiln heating elements can be readily repaired. Do not stretch or make a sharp bend in the wire as it is quite brittle. Clean off the corrosion from the existing wire and add a new piece, as at left. Mix borax with grease to make a paste, then apply it on the joints. As below, staples made of nichrome wire will hold the new section in place. The more staples you use, the stronger your splice will become.

Input Requirements

The input required for a small ceramic kiln depends primarily on size and maximum operating temperature, but also work-load, shape, insulation, etc., play an important role. Below is a table giving average inputs for ceramic kilns of different sizes operating at temperatures up to approximately 2200-2250°F.

SIZE		INPUT KW
100 Cubic Inches		0.9
200 " "		1.3
300 " "		1.6
400 " "		1.9
500 " "		2.2
1 Cubic Ft.		5.
2 " "		7.5
3 " "		9
4 " "		11.
5 " "		13.
10 " "		20.

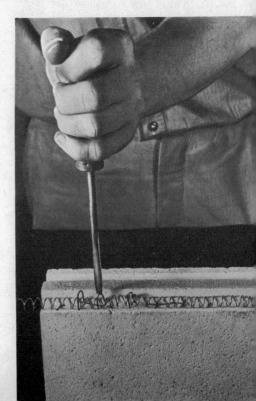

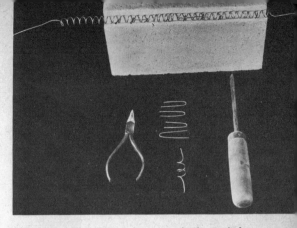

Materials and tools for making a good splice include pliers, screwdriver and nichrome wire. Nichrome, as its name implies, is a nickel-chrome alloy.

can start a fire if placed upon wood or paper. Keep hot ware out of drafts.

Should you use tongs to remove ware from the kiln, make sure that the portion of the tongs that touch the ware have been heated, too, or the ware may shatter. As you grow more experienced in kiln operation, you will develop your own technique. For example, several operators open their kiln doors as soon as all the color has disappeared. They then hasten the cooling by placing a fan on top of the kiln, blowing away from the kiln. Thermal circulation forces the hotter air up. The fan sets up a motion that blows the air away and the space occupied by this hot air is occupied by more hot air which also is blown away. This form of artificial circulation does cool down the kiln more rapidly, but cannot be employed unless the ware can stand the thermal shock. Certain clays are capable of withstanding drastic temperatures; others cannot tolerate these rapid changes. As a general rule, a thin piece of ware can better endure the stress of radically changing temperatures than can a thick piece.

In the process of bisque firing, it must be remembered that the higher the fire the more the piece shrinks and hence becomes dense and less porous. The less porous, the more difficult will be the glaze application. The lower the piece is fired within its maturity range, the more easily the glaze will adhere. This is what is designated by clay which matures at .02-.06—such clay should be bisque at .06, and the glaze fire may be as high as .02 depending upon the glaze tolerance for heat. This bisque process or heat treating of your ware renders it hard and firm, though still brittle. The bisque ware may be freely handled but will shatter much like glass if subject to shock. •

If a portion of your kiln is in need of repair, a mixture of powdered brick should be used to fill in the spots. This compound is obtainable ready-made.

KANTHAL A WIRE

Maximum wire operating temperatures: 2370°F.
Resistivity at 68°F: 836 ohms per cir. mil foot.
Specific gravity: 7.15
Weight per cubic inch: 0.258 lbs.

Factors for Determining Resistance at Various Temperatures

Temperature °C	20	100	200	300	400	500	600	700	800	900	1000	1100	1200	1300
Temperature °F	68	212	392	572	752	932	1112	1292	1472	1652	1832	2012	2192	2372
Factor	1,000	1,002	1,005	1,008	1,012	1,018	1,023	1,025	1,030	1,040	1,046	1,050	1,055	1,060

B&S	Dia. in Inches	Ohms per Ft. (68°F)	Sq. in per Ft.	Ft. per Lb.	Lbs. per M Feet	Ohms per Lb.	Sq. inches per Ohm (68°F)
10	.1019	.08051	3.842	39.61	25.24	3.189	47.72
11	.0907	.1015	3.421	49.95	20.02	5.070	33.70
12	.0808	.1280	3.046	62.97	15.88	8.060	23.79
13	.0720	.1613	2.713	79.42	12.59	12.82	16.80
14	.0641	.2036	2.416	100.1	9.984	20.38	11.86
15	.0571	.2567	2.152	126.2	7.920	32.40	8.383
16	.0508	.3237	1.916	159.2	6.281	51.53	5.919
17	.0453	.4081	1.706	200.8	4.980	81.95	4.180
18	.0403	.5148	1.519	253.2	3.949	130.4	2.950

A flat, varnish-type brush may be used to apply glaze on bisque ware. Make only one stroke with each side of the brush, then re-dip.

Glazes and How to Apply Them

If the glaze fits the body of the clay and is properly fired, you'll find that glost is an effective way of decorating ware.

THE word glaze denotes the finish deposited upon a piece of ware. It is a shiny, hard, nonporous finish, colored or colorless. Glazes may be gloss, nontransparent, such as majolica, or they may be transparent in color or without color. Glazes may also be semigloss or matt or opaque. Glazes may also be made to develop a crackle finish.

It is important to make sure that the glaze you use fits the body of the clay. If, for example, the clay body should shrink more than the glaze, the resultant ware will show signs of "shivering." Whole sections of glaze will chip or shiver off the ware. If the clay should shrink less than the glaze during firing, the finished ware might show signs of spaces between which the bisque will show. This is a form of "crazing." Often the results of unmatched body and glaze will not become noticeable until the ware has cooled to room temperature. Incorrect firing will also cause unhappy results. A glaze sold to be fired at .04 may mature at .05, but may not fit the clay body as well as if it had been fired at its pre-scribed or recommended temperature.

There are several methods of decorating a piece of ware. The easiest method is to cover the piece of bisque ware with a gloss or majolica glaze. This glaze flows out as it matures and will deposit an even, shiny finish on the ware either in colorless or colored surfacing over your entire piece.

Ware may also be decorated by the use of underglaze. This is a coloring agent resembling its true tone before firing. Underglaze colors do not flow under heat. Their application is much like the use of water color. Most underglaze colors do not need firing to set the color. They must, however, be glazed with a transparent glaze in order to preserve the color and bring out the latent beauty of many blends of underglaze colors.

All glazes contain glasslike or glass ingredients in their basic formulas. It is this that causes the glassy, shiny finish. Color is caused by metals—copper for green, cobalt for blue. And when uranium was available to the potter, our best reds were formed with uranium salts. Clay or Kaolin

Glazes may be transparent, opaque, majolica, semi-gloss or matt, as shown by varied samples, above.

Interesting mottled or striped effects can also be achieved by glost, using special glazes, techniques.

forms an important ingredient in glazes. Most glazes are dulled by the increased percentages of Kaolin. Many glazes are formed by the use of basic frits. A frit is the result of blending certain chemicals and heating them to their molten state. This mass is then dripped into water. The molten drops explode, upon touching water, into crystals, which are then ground or pulverized to a fine powder—usually between 250 and 400 mesh. The use of various formulas causes certain results when mill additions are blended with the frit. It is by using certain frits that crackle finishes or icelike finishes, or bubble finish are obtained. One of the most popular frits for the hobbyist to use, and one which is also used by many industrial houses producing pottery for market use, is sold by two large chemical houses. Frit No. G24 is an excellent frit for good results in making your own glaze. This frit is sold in small quantities at an advanced price, but in 100 pound lots its cost is much lower.

There is virtually no limit to the shapes and the color-combinations that can be achieved by glazing.

Color may be added directly to the glaze body. For an opaque glaze, add Ferro white stain, as shown.

How to Prepare a Glaze

In preparing a clear transparent glaze, use nine parts Frit No. G24 and one part EPK or Georgia clay (which is Kaolin). To this mixture add about 2 percent ordinary household borax. This will aid the glaze in flowing more evenly when fired in your kiln. This glaze should be fired at cone .05, or .04 at the highest.

If you wish to make your own colored glaze you may use this same clear glaze and add glaze stains in proportion to your need for depth of color 2-20%. This writer suggests that liquid stains such as Ferro's liquid stain should be used to color your clear glaze since this material is already milled and readily mixes with your clear glaze by merely stirring in a liquid solution about the consistency of light cream. A decided advantage is that while there are many Ferro colors available, they can be further mixed with each other to produce many shades and blends. This permits the

Make a color chart of your favorite colors by firing them on a single tile, labeling clearly.

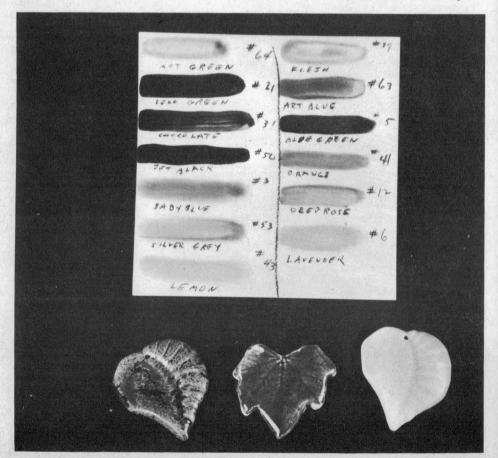

hobbyist to develop his own distinctive colors. All of these glazes can be made opaque by adding your own white glaze or Ferro white stain to your prepared colored glaze. The white acts as an opaquifier. About 10% white glaze added to your colored glaze will be adequate for opaque glaze. The white will change the shade of your colored glaze, and more stain may be required to maintain your desired shade.

In discussing glazes, it is necessary to touch on stone glazes and antiques. Stone glazes are glazes which are fired to high temperatures on clay bodies which will withstand such temperatures. The finish is matt and opaque. Somewhat the same finish is accomplished by the use of rutile or antique glazes. Antique glazes are unusual in their effect, as they develop shades of the basic color of your ware and there are usually mottlings of gold and brown or other contrasts shot throughout the finish. The final appearance discloses that most of the surface is matt and opaque, though there will also be blends of gloss opaque color on the ware, too. These glazes are available in at least a dozen colors.

Three Lions

Most glaze recipes require a scrupulous weighing of ingredients so that true colors are reproduced.

At right, pestle and mortar operation is employed by the hobbyist to satisfactorily mix glaze colors.

COLORLESS AND WHITE GLAZES

Clear—Cone 014-3

Molecular Compositions (Equivalents)

	No. 1	No. 2	No. 3
$KNaO$	.2	.2	.2
CaO	.1	.1	.1
SrO	.3	.4	.5
BaO	.4	.3	.2
Al_2O_3	.3	.3	.3
SiO_1	3.0	3.0	3.0
B_2O_3	.3	.3	.3

Melted Compositions

	No. 1	No. 2	No. 3
$KNaO$	4.52%	4.59%	4.65%
CaO	1.62	1.65	1.67
SrO	8.99	12.17	15.44
BaO	17.77	13.52	9.14
Al_2O_3	8.85	8.98	9.11
SiO_2	52.20	52.97	53.74
B_2O_3	6.04	6.13	6.22

Batch Compositions

Frits	No. 1	No. 2	No. 3
Nepheline syenite	23.20%	23.48%	23.81%
Pyrophyllite	5.50	5.56	5.65
Flint	27.60	27.95	28.34
Strontium carbonate	11.38	15.36	10.41
Barium carbonate	20.25	15.40	19.45
Boric acid	9.54	9.65	9.77
Whiting	2.49	2.60	2.64
Glazes			
Frit	97.76	97.74	97.70
Clay	2.24	2.26	2.30

Three Lions

Below, glaze in liquid form is sprayed on bisque by power equipment. Be sure spray area is ventilated.

Three Lions

Recipes for Low-Temperature Glazes

Rock Green
Litharge 720
Flint 200
Kaolin 80
Copper Carbonate .. 30
Pyrolusite 5

Light Green
Red Lead 700
Flint 220
Kaolin 80
Iron Oxide (red) ... 10
Copper Oxide 10

Reseda Green
Litharge 720
Flint 210
Kaolin 70
Smalte 40
Iron Oxide (red) ... 10

Yellow Green
Litharge 720
Kaolin 70
Flint 210
Chrome Oxide 3
Copper Carbonate .. 12

Apple Green
Litharge 700
Kaolin 100
Flint 200
Iron Oxide (red) ... 8
Copper Oxide 8

Grey Green
Litharge 710
Kaolin 90
Flint 200
Iron Oxide (red) ... 10
Manganese Dioxide .. 10

Emerald Green
Litharge 710
Kaolin 90
Flint 200
Copper Oxide 30
Chrome Oxide 1

Soft Green
Litharge 700
Kaolin 100
Flint 200
Copper Oxide 25
Iron Oxide (red) ... 20

Light May Green
Litharge 740
Kaolin 60
Flint 200
Nickel Oxide (green) . 2
Chrome Oxide 1
Copper Carbonate .. 5

Light Green
Litharge 700
Flint 150
Feldspar 70
Kaolin 80
Copper Oxide 3
Manganese Dioxide .. 2
Iron Oxide 2

Grass Green
Litharge 720
Kaolin 70
Flint 210
Copper Carbonate .. 8
Iron Oxide (red) ... 1
Manganese Dioxide .. 1

Moon Green
Litharge 720
Flint 210
Kaolin 70
Nickel Oxide (green) . 7
Manganese Dioxide .. 6

Sea Green
Litharge 720
Flint 200
Kaolin 80
Smalte 4
Iron Oxide (red) ... 5
Copper Carbonate .. 7

Leaf Green
Litharge 720
Sand 210
Kaolin 70
Lead Chromate 2
Manganese Dioxide .. 4
Smalte 1

Wood Green
Litharge 700
Flint 120
Kaolin 60
Feldspar 120
Copper Oxide 26
Manganese Dioxide .. 9

Moss Green
Litharge 740
Flint 200
Kaolin 60
Iron Oxide (black) .. 20
Copper Oxide 20
Chrome Oxide 2
Manganese Dioxide .. 5

Bronze Green (light)
Litharge 740
Flint 200
Kaolin 60
Chrome Oxide 2
Copper Carbonate .. 7
Manganese Dioxide .. 3
Iron Oxide (black) .. 3

Bronze Green (dark)
Litharge 730
Flint 200
Kaolin 70
Copper Oxide 20
Iron Oxide (black) .. 10
Manganese Dioxide .. 10
Chrome Oxide 2

Blue Green
Litharge 700
Flint 200
Kaolin 100
Copper Carbonate .. 15
Cobalt Carbonate ... 5

Molachite Green
Litharge 700
Kaolin 100
Flint 200
Copper Carbonate .. 17

Yellow Green
Litharge 740
Flint 200
Kaolin 60
Lead Chromate 10
Copper Oxide 4
Smalte 3

Turkish Green
Frit 60:
Litharge 130
Flint 40
Borax 120
Whiting 10
Glaze:
Frit 60 230
Kaolin 20
Zinc Oxide 10
Feldspar 12
Copper Carbonate .. 4

Grass Green
Litharge 740
Flint 200
Kaolin 60
Copper Oxide 30
Lead Chromate 2

Light Brown Green
Litharge 740
Flint 200
Kaolin 60
Copper Oxide 8
Iron Oxide (red) ... 10
Pyrolusite 3

Brown Green
Litharge 740
Flint 200
Kaolin 60
Copper Oxide 10
Chrome Oxide 2
Pyrolusite 10

Black Green
Litharge 740
Flint 200
Kaolin 60
Iron Oxide (black) .. 10
Copper Oxide 25
Manganese Carbonate 10

Grey Green
Red Lead 740
Flint 260
Kaolin 80
Copper Oxide 9
Manganese Carbonate 5
Tin Oxide 4

Rock Green
Litharge 730
Flint 200
Kaolin 70
Lead Chromate 3
Manganese Carbonate 3
Smalte 4

Water Green
Litharge 740
Flint 200
Kaolin 60
Manganese Carbonate 1
Cobalt Oxide 2
Iron Oxide (black) ... 3

Mignonette Green
Litharge 730
Flint 200
Kaolin 70
Smalte 50
Iron Oxide (black) ... 20

Light Blue
Litharge 700
Spar 250
Kaolin 50
Copper Carbonate .. 3
Cobalt Carbonate ... 5
Ferruginous Clay ... 4

Medium Blue
Litharge 700
Flint 200
Kaolin 100
Cobalt Carbonate ... 20

Violet Blue
Litharge 700
Flint 200
Kaolin 100
Cobalt Carbonate ... 10
Manganese Dioxide .. 15

Indigo Blue
Litharge 700
Flint 200
Kaolin 100
Cobalt 15
Pyrolusite 10
Iron Oxide 2

Purple Blue
Litharge 700
Kaolin 100
Flint 200
Cobalt Carbonate ... 16
Manganese Dioxide .. 8

Water Blue
Litharge 700
Flint 150
Kaolin 60
Feldspar 90
Smalte 2

Green Blue
Red Lead 700
Flint 200
Kaolin 100
Smalte 100
Copper Oxide 5
Iron Oxide (red) 3

Heaven Blue
Litharge 700
Flint 50
Kaolin 50
Feldspar 290
Cobalt Oxide 8
Copper Oxide 15

Violet Blue

Frit 62:
Red Lead	670
Borax	1500
Whiting	200
Fluorspar	60
Flint	840

Glaze:
Frit 62	960
Kaolin	50
Manganese Dioxide	20
Cobalt Carbonate	13

Azure Blue
Frit 62	100
Kaolin	15
Cobalt Carbonate	1
Copper Carbonate	10

Sky Blue
Frit 60	230
Kaolin	20
Zinc Oxide	10
Feldspar	10
Copper Carbonate	5
Cobalt Carbonate	5

Dark Blue
Litharge	700
Flint	200
Kaolin	100
Cobalt Oxide	20

Black Blue
Litharge	700
Flint	200
Kaolin	100
Cobalt Oxide	15
Manganese Carbonate	8
Iron Oxide (black)	5

Indigo
Litharge	740
Flint	200
Kaolin	60
Copper Oxide	8
Cobalt Oxide	10

Orange Brown
Litharge	700
Flint	200
Kaolin	100
Iron Oxide	30
Pyrolusite	10

Wood Brown
Litharge	740
Flint	190
Kaolin	70
Manganese Dioxide	30
Iron Oxide (red)	10

Dark Brown
Litharge	730
Kaolin	70
Flint	200
Manganese Dioxide	15
Lead Chromate	15

Coffee Brown
Litharge	720
Kaolin	70
Flint	210
Nickel Oxide (green)	12
Manganese Dioxide	5

Liver Brown
Litharge	740
Flint	200
Kaolin	60
Tin Oxide	35
Pyrolusite	15
Iron Oxide	5

Plum Brown
Litharge	700
Kaolin	100
Flint	200
Lead Chromate	12
Manganese Dioxide	8

Malt Brown
Red Lead	740
Flint	100
Kaolin	60
Feldspar	100
Manganese Dioxide	20
Iron Oxide (black)	15
Copper Oxide	7

Yellow Brown
Litharge	740
Flint	200
Kaolin	60
Iron Oxide (red)	20
Manganese Dioxide	10

Nut Brown
Litharge	740
Flint	200
Kaolin	60
Pyrolusite	20
Iron Oxide (black)	5
Cobalt Oxide	5

Dusky Brown
Litharge	740
Flint	200
Kaolin	60
Lead Chromate	5
Manganese Carbonate	5
Smalte	1

Mulberry Brown
Litharge	700
Feldspar	180
Flint	70
Kaolin	50
Manganese Carbonate	25

Green Brown
Litharge	720
Flint	200
Kaolin	80
Lead Chromate	4
Manganese Carbonate	3
Smalte	3

Red Brown
Litharge	750
Flint	200
Kaolin	50
Iron Oxide (black)	10
Manganese Carbonate	10
Zinc Oxide	10

Mulberry Violet
Frit 60	230
Kaolin	20
Feldspar	5
Manganese Dioxide	2
Cobalt Carbonate	6

Black Violet
Litharge	750
Flint	200
Kaolin	50
Pyrolusite	28
Cobalt Oxide	8
Copper Oxide	8

Violet
Red Lead	700
Flint	50
Kaolin	50
Feldspar	200
Cobalt Oxide	1
Manganese Dioxide	1

Pale Yellow
Red Lead	680
Zinc Oxide	60
Flint	180
Kaolin	80
Rutile	2

Straw Color
Litharge	700
Flint	100
Kaolin	50
Feldspar	150
Nickel Oxide (green)	7

Bronze
Litharge	720
Flint	200
Kaolin	80
Lead Chromate	8
Pyrolusite	4
Iron Oxide	4

Flesh Color
Red Lead	70
Feldspar	30
Manganese Dioxide	2

Pale Rose
Frit 62	960
Kaolin	50
Manganese Dioxide	1

Moonlight Clear
Litharge	700
Zinc Oxide	60
Flint	200
Kaolin	60

Apple Grey
Litharge	700
Flint	200
Kaolin	100
Pyrolusite	1
Copper Oxide	5

Dawn Grey
Litharge	740
Flint	200
Kaolin	60
$CuCO_3$	6
Pyrolusite	5
Cobalt Carbonate	2

Violet Grey
Litharge	720
Flint	200
Kaolin	80
Cobalt	3
Iron Oxide	1
Pyrolusite	7

Straw Grey
Litharge	720
Kaolin	80
Flint	200
Manganese Dioxide	8
Copper Oxide	4
Cobalt Carbonate	1
Iron Oxide (red)	2

Stone Grey
Litharge	720
Flint	200
Kaolin	80
Copper Carbonate	5
Manganese Dioxide	8
Cobalt Oxide	1

Dove Grey
Red Lead	700
Flint	120
Kaolin	60
Feldspar	120
Tin Oxide	25
Manganese Dioxide	6
Cobalt Carbonate	4

Blue Grey
Litharge	740
Flint	200
Kaolin	60
Manganese Dioxide	7
Cobalt Oxide	7
Iron Oxide (black)	3

Turkish Blue Grey
Frit 62	960
Kaolin	50
Manganese Dioxide	3
Copper Carbonate	15

Platinum Grey
Litharge	760
Flint	180
Kaolin	60
Manganese Carbonate	3
Cobalt Oxide	1
Iron Oxide (black)	1

Black
Litharge	720
Flint	200
Kaolin	80
Cobalt Oxide	30
Manganese Dioxide	30
Iron Oxide (red)	20

Brown Black
Litharge	740
Flint	200
Kaolin	60
Pyrolusite	30
Cobalt Oxide	5
Iron Oxide	10
Copper Oxide	10

Blue Black
Litharge	740
Flint	200
Kaolin	60
Cobalt	30
Iron Oxide	15
Pyrolusite	15

Glaze Application

There are many methods of applying glaze. It is important to remember when you glaze a piece of ware that you are coating your clay with powdered colored glass ingredients suspended in water. Color will only appear where it is applied. It is true that glazes flow out to even themselves when heated, much like enamel. However, unlike enamel, they will not necessarily flow over a bare spot to fully hide it. Glaze cannot be used to hide a blemish; it will accentuate errors rather than conceal them.

The normal technique is first to make your piece, and when it is completely air-dried, fire it. When it has been removed from the kiln, it may be glazed in any of the following manners:

The glaze solution is blended to about

In brushing on glaze, apply second coat at right angles to first one. The third coat is made diagonally.

the consistency of light cream. A flat, varnish-type brush about ¾″ wide is used to apply the glaze finish on the piece of ware, and it is applied in the following manner: the brush is dipped into the liquid and the excess liquid is *not* scraped from the brush. Make one stroke only with each side of the brush, of not more than three inches in length, then re-dip brush. The strokes are made in one direction. The bottom of the piece is not glazed. When the glaze has dried, a second coat is applied in exactly the same manner. These strokes are at right angles to the first strokes. When the second coat is dried, a third coat is applied using strokes on the diagonal so that they are in still a different direction from that of the first or second coat. When the piece has dried thoroughly, it is ready to be put into the kiln. Drying time should be about 24 hours. Glazed ware should not touch either kiln walls or any other piece of material in the kiln.

If enough pieces are to be glazed in the same color it would be sensible to mix sufficient glaze solution, making your solution slightly thinner, and dipping the entire piece. One immersion is sufficient.

The third method would be to make your glaze solution as thin as milk and pour the solution into the barrel of an insecticide gun and spray the object with this solution. Three applications of spray will be necessary. Spraying should be done out of doors since most glazes contain lead and other toxic ingredients.

There are specialized applications of glaze which are widely used; one such method consists of holding the piece over the bowl of glaze and scooping the liquid glaze up with one hand and pouring the glaze out of the hand onto the piece, allowing the excess glaze to drip back into the bowl. When the piece has been thoroughly covered it is set down on a stilt and the parts of ware that have been unglazed due to the hand marks in holding the piece are then glazed with a brush.

Certain materials blister or bubble when heated. Most of these will respond to a second firing to correct such faults. Manganese and sulfur are the most prominent of this group of chemicals. Frequently a glaze will flow well during the firing, but the color does not; this is often true of pastels. You can overcome this by more thorough mixing of the glaze before and during application. A piece may be re-glazed many times and refired, even changing the glaze. It will be hard to apply glaze to a glazed surface, however. The best procedure is to heat your piece to about 125-150 degrees Fahrenheit and apply your glaze thickly to the heated ware. This will evaporate the water quickly and allow the glaze to remain deposited on the ware. Be sure to use plenty of gum for this application, however, for best results.

Your piece should not be glazed on the underside—or at least it should have an unglazed footing.

At left, dip method may also be used for glazing, but be sure solution is thin enough. This speeds up production where quantities are involved, as one dip is enough. Dip solution may also be sprayed with ordinary hand sprayer (center) or scooped up and poured over the piece (right) and finished with brush.

Before glaze firing, paint kiln furniture with a mixture of powdered flint and Kaolin (kiln wash) so that drippings from ware do not mar your kiln.

Many ceramists glaze the underside of ware to make it watertight. If this is done use stilts that have wire supports made of heat-resistant nichrome wire.

Stilts as well as shelves should be treated with a coat of kiln wash. This solution is actually clay which will not mature at the temperatures you use.

Glost or Glaze Firing

In order to prepare for the glaze fire, or glost, as it is technically known, there are certain basic rules which are common sense. Remembering that glaze will flow when heated in the kiln, care must be exercised to prevent molten glaze from dripping on a shelf or other ware, or even on a stilt point.

The preparation used for this purpose is called "kiln wash." Kiln wash is prepared by mixing 50% powdered flint and 50% Kaolin. Any Kaolin will suffice. These two ingredients should be thoroughly mixed and stirred in water to the consistency of cream. Paint the floor of your kiln, one side of your shelves, your shelf supports or posts, and your stilt points with kiln wash. Kiln wash is actually slip made of a clay which will not mature at your kiln temperature, hence it can be scraped off with no difficulty, and with it will come any glaze which has dripped. Kiln wash should be used before each glaze firing. Should the wash begin to build up an appreciable thickness, scrape it all off and apply fresh wash.

In preparing to stack for glost fire, place your thinner ware on the bottom of the kiln, just the reverse of the bisque fire. The hottest area will provide the best soak-ing position, since heavy ware will require more heat soaking than thin ware. Place your thinnest ware on the floor of the kiln, being sure to set each glazed piece on its own stilt. Allow no piece to touch any other piece, or any part of the kiln. No glazed piece should be glazed on the bottom, but many ceramists frequently glaze all over in order to render a dish or a vase water-tight. In the event you are trying to stilt such a piece, use a star stilt. These are stilts with short heat-resistant wire prongs projecting upwards. This allows less contact points than regular stilts.

You may make your own star stilts easily by cutting a small piece of the insulating brick of the type used in making the kiln. The average size piece should be ½" thick, 1" wide, 2" long. Into this block push three pieces of high temperature wire, the type used to make your kiln element. Do not allow more than ¼" or ⅜" of wire to project upward. The pieces of wire are placed in position to provide three contact points with the ware.

If you have enough ware and space in the kiln to employ the use of a shelf or shelves, place your posts or shelf supports on the floor of the kiln preparatory to stacking your first level. This will avoid the frustration which follows when your floor is fully stacked and you realize you have forgotten to put in your posts.

Try to keep each level of your kiln stacked with pieces of the same height. This will enable you to get the most out of your kiln area. Follow the aforementioned procedure throughout the stacking of your kiln, shelf by shelf. When the kiln is ready to fire, you need not fire your glaze ware as slowly as bisque ware, since the clay has already been fired. The procedure should be as follows:

Turn the kiln on low heat throughout the entire area and allow the door to remain open for 15 minutes; then turn to high heat, allowing the door to remain open for another 15 minutes. Now shut the door tightly. Do not jar or shake the kiln, as the pieces are balanced on stilts and may tip. Remember, any glazed piece will adhere to anything it touches when exposed to heat. Also bear in mind that any piece overhanging a shelf may drip glaze on the piece beneath.

When your cone has begun to bend over, shut off the kiln. Allow the kiln to cool thoroughly before opening, as drafts on most glazeware will cause crazing. The usual cycle of twice the heating time is required for cooling. Your cone or maturity temperature will have a direct bearing on your glaze. Underfired ware appears milky or not shiny, nor does it flow properly. Overfiring causes much of the glaze to run off the piece and leave the top or upper portion nearly unglazed. Antique glazes which develop too much shine or gloss should be fired higher. A piece of ware not fired satisfactorily may be glazed and fired again. However, you will find that the glaze solution will not adhere well on the surface. Four or five coats may be necessary in order to get a heavy enough coat of glaze on an already glazed surface. Another condition which may cause a problem and which often occurs is blistering. This is frequently sulfur or manganese, which may be used in certain glazes. These blisters will fire out if the piece is refired with no additional glaze added.

Glaze applied heavily usually drips off a piece of ware during the glost fire. Some of this molten matter clings to the bottom of the clay and cools, leaving hangings much like icicles. These pieces must be removed from the ware before it can be considered finished. Such glaze may be ground off by using a carborundum wheel or a file. Always grind so that your wheel is cutting toward the center of the bottom of the ware, as the glaze may chip off and it will flake in the direction of stress. In this direction the ware itself will be unblemished.

The advantage of kiln furniture is that it allows you to use all of your available kiln space. Here are shelves, supports and a rack for firing tiles.

In glaze firing, reverse bisque firing procedure and put the thinnest ware on the bottom. Be sure that all pieces are placed on supporting stilts.

Sometimes glaze drips off and leaves a hanging. It may be removed by a file or carborundum wheel but grind so wheel cuts toward center of piece.

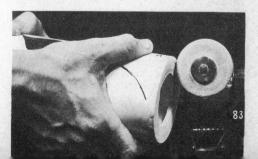

83

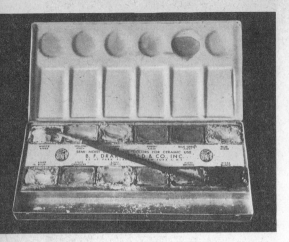

Underglaze

As previously mentioned, underglaze resembles its actual color before firing. In preparing a piece for underglaze application there are not too many rules, since underglaze decoration may be applied while the ware is plastic, leather hard, bone dry, or bisque. The ware should be fettled and wiped off with a sponge to remove any dust. The only objection to applying underglaze on a plastic piece is the tendency of the thin color to run. Most hobbyists decorate a bone dry or bisque piece. Under these conditions the designer may outline his decoration with a pencil, as such marks will burn off in the kiln.

Underglaze color is prepared in cake form similar to dry water colors. It is also prepared in a thick liquid to be thinned before use. Some underglaze colors are ready prepared in the proper consistency, ready for use. Basically, underglaze stains are a powder which requires preparation for use.

In using the pallet form of underglazes, care must be exercised in that a moist brush should be applied to the pallet and then used to design the ware. Each stroke mark may show since, like water color, repetitious brushing or pressure on the bristles or the amount of water used, changes the color intensity and does tend to leave brush marks. If this type of underglaze is used, it is better to place a little water in the pan on the cover of the pallet box or on a piece of glass. Then with your brush, deposit color in the water to get the shade desired. Using this liquid color, you will at least have a source of color of the same intensity. However, attention must be paid to the number of coats you apply.

In preparing your own underglaze, your medium is important. Glycerine and gum mixed, act as excellent mediums or vehicles, since they help the color to flow smoothly off the brush. To make a simple but effective underglaze, this writer has found that Ferro liquid stains will tolerate high temperatures. These are the same stains recommended for the color addition to the fritted clear glaze. This stain is too thick to use "as is" for underglaze, since it is far too viscous. It may be thinned with water for application as an underglaze, but thinning to a proper consistency by the use of a solution of gum arabic and gum tragacanth is better. A few drops of glycerine to a liquid ounce of color will also aid the flowing of the color during application. If brush marks show, add 10% clear glaze solution to your underglaze by volume. This will act as a flux while firing in the kiln and tend to even out your color.

Most underglazes, particularly those mentioned herein, will blend. This is not true of most manufactured glazes. You will be able to blend and make your own shades of both glaze and underglaze using the formula herein mentioned.

Do not expect your underglaze to express true color until after clear glaze application and firing. This final treatment brings forth the hidden beauty of a dull color, much as shellac or clear varnish brings out the lustre of water color. Application should be brushed on with a regular water color brush (size based upon the design to be painted). After the underglaze color has dried thoroughly, the ware should be clear glazed, which is best done by spraying. The spray method seldom deposits enough water on the ware to allow the underglaze color to run. Too much liquid applied over underglaze will allow the pigment to "weep." This will spoil your design. Certain colors will flow when the clear glaze over them is heated. Sometimes this condition can be overcome by firing your underglazed ware before the application of clear glaze. If the condition persists, a clear glaze which will not drag your particular color must be used. Sometimes a transparent glaze made without zinc will qualify in this respect, or perhaps a transparent clear glaze made without lead will suffice. These conditions, however, seldom occur when you use a fritted clear glaze, if not too moist.

After your color and transparent glaze has been applied, allow your piece to dry thoroughly. While it is drying, keep it free from dust and grit. If the ware has not been bisqued, fire slowly. If the piece has been bisqued, follow the rules for glost fire.

Common Glazing Faults

If glaze chips off a piece of bisque ware while cooling, it is an indication that the bodies do not fit. The clay body is contracted more than the glaze; thus, upon cooling the hard glassy surface is chipping or peeling away from the body of the ware. If the glaze can be made to mature at a lower temperature by adding borax to the glaze, or if a clay with a lower maturing temperature is used, less shrinkage of the clay will take place.

Peeling, too, is caused by the same condition, but may also be caused by too heavy a coat of underglaze on the ware, to which has been added a heavy coat of clear glaze. Thinner applications of decorative material will correct this.

Crazing is one of the common faults disclosed by too rapid cooling of a piece of ware, or unmatched bodies. If the glaze shrinks more than the body during firing and subsequent cooling, crazing will occur. Usually, a higher bisque fire will shrink the ware so that it will hold the glaze without crazing. Particularly is this true of Jordan and Monmouth clays. These clays will tolerate 2100 degrees Fahrenheit, but here you must be sure your glaze, too, will stand such temperature without losing its color. Ordinary white clays designed to reach no higher than cone .02 may have their maturity temperature raised by adding 2% more flint to the body. If you remember that practical common sense plays an important part in determining the cause of these errors, correction will be easy. These rules are of prime importance:

1. The higher the temperature, the greater the shrinkage of both clay and glaze.

2. Flint added to most bodies increases the maturity temperature.

3. Borax, when added to most bodies, decreases the maturity temperature.

Hence, by examination you can determine which caused damage—the shrinkage of clay or of glaze, and by the application of these rules correct your material. •

When a glaze does not fit the clay body, the ware will contract more than the glaze, causing chips.

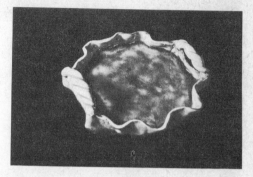

Fine hairline cracks in a glaze is called crazing. This may develop in a piece even after its firing.

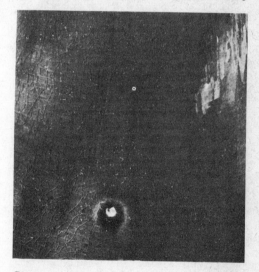

Crazing may be combined with blistering or "shivering" in which bumps and contusions mar a glaze.

Where too heavy a glaze is used, surface markings will appear. Correct this by using a thinner glaze.

Below, too much underglaze on the ware causes the piece to peel. Whole sections of glaze may be lost.

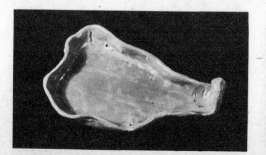

Tiles and Dinnerware

Decorative as well as dutiful, this form of ceramic design

appeals to the hobbyist as an inspiration—and a challenge.

MANY forms of tile decoration are now being developed throughout the United States. All gift shops feature the use of tiles for coasters or for a continuous design, i.e. a group of tiles set together in a picture frame or a table top as though the group of tiles were one unbroken surface. This type of decorative ware is extremely pleasing to the eye, and used as a table top or tray is a useful addition to the home. Tile tops for trays or tables will not be affected by hot dishes placed upon them, nor will they stain from liquids.

Commercial tiles are manufactured by several large tile companies whose facilities permit them to make a tile for resale for little more than the cost of the material.

The chief difference between the homemade tile and the industrially made tile is uniformity. Tile plants roll or extrude their moist clay under extreme pressure, which is uniform at all times. The shape is cut and pressed under large hydraulic presses. The tile is also fired under pressure. It is these processes which keep the tile from warping visibly.

The hobbyist, too, may make fairly accurate tiles by rolling out clay on the reverse side of a piece of oilcloth. Roll out to the desired thickness of your tile. Use a straightedged right angle to mark a true square to the size you desire. Cut with a sharp knife. Allow to dry slowly on a plaster bat. Weight the tile during the drying

Tiles for decorating may be obtained already bisque fired in various sizes or they may be made by the ceramist, the difference being greater uniformity. Above are three steps in decorating a tile. At left the pattern is traced on in pencil, then glazed in (center) and finally ready to fire, as at the right.

process, as this will help it to remain flat. It may still warp during the firing, however. This can be minimized if you place the tile between two shelves which will bear directly below and above the tile while being fired. Tiles are available commercially in bisque or glazed state. They may be bought directly from the manufacturer in cartons. The manufacturer may restrict such sales to not less than three cartons at a time. The number of tiles in a carton varies.

(6"x6" squares and 6-inch circles are packed 90 tiles to a carton, while the 6"x4¼" oblong or ellipse tiles are packed 126 pieces to the carton. 4¼"x4¼" tiles with plain or raised border are packed 180 pieces to a carton). Any of the foregoing shapes may be made by the hobbyist. The round tiles are made by using a divider to scribe a circle to the diameter you desire. Then the focal point at the center is filled to remove the mark of your divider. Cut

Tracing paper may be used to transfer a design to the tile, since pencil marks will be burned out when the piece is fired. The lines of the tracing are brought up before the glaze is applied. Tiles may be decorated with overglaze colors as well, but such designs should be applied to previously glazed tiles.

For overglaze decoration, you will need the proper tools, which include brushes, knives, a glass pallet, pencils and a banding wheel.

The banding wheel, while not essential to an overglaze design, is a must for getting clean lines around your ware. Use a steady motion. Below, a vase is being decorated by overglaze. The advantage of this medium is that it renders a design impervious to handling.

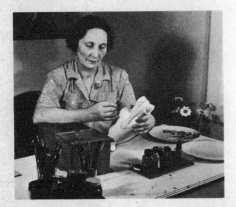

your score mark with a sharp knife and trim the edges. Allow to dry the same as the square tile. Those tiles with raised edges require a different procedure. These must be made by first making the shape you desire from a block of plaster. Then, using this as your master mold, cast a one-piece press mold.

Dinnerware, too, has much beauty when decorated nicely, as well as utility. Plates, cups, platters, hors d'oeuvres dishes and the whole gamut of table utensils will inspire the hobbyist. Dishes may be purchased either bisque or glazed from nearly any pottery manufacturing dinnerware. Such ware as unglazed or bisque tile or dinnerware should be sponged and decorated with underglaze color, much the same as regular underglaze decoration. You may, if you wish, outline your design in pencil, as this outline will burn out in the firing. True color will not develop unless the piece is clear-glazed and fired.

Tiles and dinnerware may also be decorated by the use of overglaze colors. These are pigments which will tolerate fairly high temperatures, ranging from .013-.018. The pigments are very similar to oil colors and are suspended in oil or turpentine. They are applied only on glazed ware. The purpose of the decorating glaze fire is to set the color, and also to permit the color to sink below the skin of the surface glaze. This process does not entirely allow the overglaze design to submerge beneath the glossy exterior, but sets the finish so as to render the ware impervious to numerous washings and wear. Such overglaze work may be performed on ware you have made yourself and clear-glazed and fired, or you may work upon tile which you have purchased already glazed. Dinnerware, too, can be bought glazed but blank of any design. Such overglaze work, of course, is done in mass production by the use of decal or by the use of rubber stamps. The rubber stamp is pressed upon a pad of overglaze, and then brought into contact with the glazed surface of the ware. Possibly three or four such patterns in different colors are so impressed for an intricate pattern. This method provides a means of mass production with economical labor.

The making of tiles and dinnerware is one of the more satisfying processes of the ceramist's art, and the design and coloring of what you produce is limited only by your own originality. As in other branches of craftwork, the free style of the individual creator imparts a distinction to the finished work not found in rigidly patterned products, so here is an opportunity to really develop along artistic lines. •

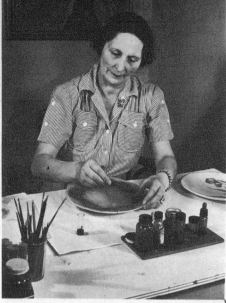

How to Overglaze Dinnerware

Exact copies of your design are required for dinnerware, so lay a perforated sheet with your decoration on it over plate, as above, then apply charcoal to the design.

At right, the outline of the design is picked up with a pencil to make it more convenient to follow when the overglaze colors are applied to the glazed plate.

An armrest and a banding wheel make the work faster and simpler. Be sure to let one color dry thoroughly before applying others near it, to avoid running.

Free-hand designs are always attractive, give your dinnerware individuality. Blank and glazed dishes may be purchased ready for patterns you choose.

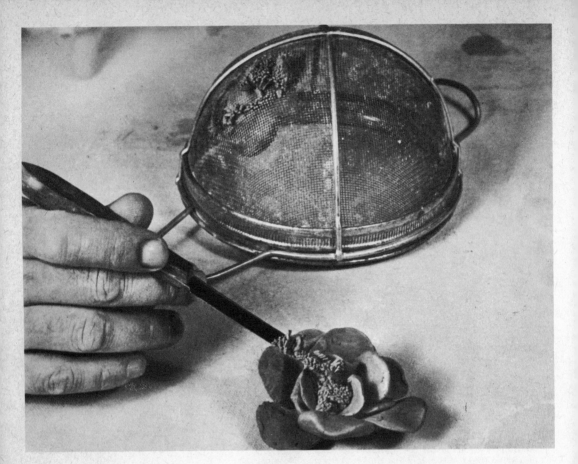

Jewelry and Lacework

Buttons and bows, pins, earrings and ornaments of all kinds

are rich rewards for this skilled ceramist's "feat of clay."

CERAMIC jewelry and lace work are among the most highly prized exhibits of skill. Certainly the reader has seen small figurines with lace or net skirts or other decorations of net, which have commanded a high price across the counter. Many such figurines are cast by the mold method.

When the piece has begun to set, it is time to be prepared to apply net or lace decoration. The first step is to measure out the amount of lace you will require. Be sure that your lace pattern is not out of proportion with the size piece you are going to decorate. Decide how you will place your lace on the figure. Wet your lace and wring it out. Dip it into slip. Draw the lace between the fingers to remove slip from the holes, or lay your wet lace upon a

piece of glass after dipping into slip. Allow it to stand a moment, then pick it up and most of the slip from the holes will remain on the glass. Now drape your lace or net, as planned, about the figure. Should any holes remain filled with slip, punch them through by using a needle. Should the lace appear not fully covered with slip, go over the lace with a brush thoroughly, wet first with water and then with slip.

Lace is extremely fragile when bisqued and if it is to be decorated with underglaze, extreme care must be exercised to prevent casualty. The glaze application should be by spray or by dip. A brush application may injure the fine lace or net. Actually, in firing the lace, all the fabric will burn out, leaving the design tracing in the slip that adhered to the cotton. This

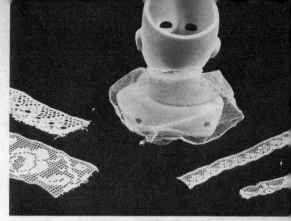

Floral designs are always interesting and not too difficult to make, with a little practice. A good idea is to use real flowers and leaves as models.

Lacework is easier than it looks. Just dip a piece of lace in slip, see that it is well distributed, then fire. The lace will burn out and clay will remain.

gossamer of clay cannot tolerate any abuse. After the glaze has been applied, fire it with extreme care. The glaze will add strength to the net. It will still be fragile, but not nearly so delicate as before glost fire.

A paper doilie may be used in much the same way to decorate an ash tray or a cigaret box. The coarser the body of the material to be burned out, the more durable will be the ware. This type of ware may also be treated with overglaze decoration. For this treatment, the ware should be bisqued, and dipped in or sprayed with clear glaze, then decorated with china paints and fired to the maturity temperature of these china paints.

Jewelry

Jewelry of all kinds can be fashioned from clay. Beads, rings, pins, earrings, charms in miniature for a bracelet, ceramic buttons for ornamentation. Small flowers provide excellent foundations for earrings. Many pieces of ceramic jewelry are fashioned from nature. Copies of shells, of small clover leaves are typical. The important points in dealing with jewelry making are enumerated herein:

1. Make sure the back is unglazed.
2. Make sure the back is smooth.
3. Cement your findings (earring backs) or pin backs or button loops only after the piece is bisqued.
4. Make matching pieces in earrings and pins in same design and in proportion—in coloring.
5. Pieces of matched color should be glazed at the same time and fired in

Below, various stages of flower-making are shown. A ball of clay (lower right) is flattened to make a petal, each petal is overlapped to shape the rose.

The stamen of the rose requires a bit of trickery. Force a lump of clay through a strainer and pick up enough of it with a thin knife to go into the bud.

91

Above are representative types of jewelry that can be made of clay. A shows earrings (top) with matching buttons below. The heart-shaped items are a set of earrings
with matching brooch. At B are flower-design earrings with matching or complementary pins. Backs should be left unglazed so that pins can be glued on. At C
are pendants made with a cookie-cutter, with loop added and tiny flowers fired on.
D shows another set of earrings with brooch to match. When making sets like this,
glaze and fire the pieces at the same time and in the same section of your kiln.

C

D

the same firing at approximately the same location in the kiln.

6. Beads should be strung on a wire for the glaze fire. This wire should be Kanthal A-1 or nichrome. The wire should be smaller than the hole in the bead to permit shrinkage.

7. Beads should not be dipped, as this will fill the holes with glaze and the beads will then stick to the wire.

8. Wire for firing must be suspended and stiff enough not to sag under heat. Beads so strung must be separated to prevent sticking together when fired.

Small, fine pieces need special tools. A wooden match stick or an orange stick with a darning needle taped along side to form a miniature sticker or a chicken quill will prove useful.

Most small objects are formed by slapping a small ball between the hands. These discs so formed will have thin edges and yet be fairly thick by comparison in their center portions. This is the starting shape for flowers, shells, buttons, leaves, and small plants. Much can be added to small ware and jewelry by the coil method. Such items as a ribbon pin are formed by coils. A bow and arrow for a brooch is made also by the coil method. Much filagree ware is fashioned by coil work.

Texture on your ware can be varied by brushing the surface with a stiff brush or scratching it with a comb.

A dishrag lightly pressed upon the clay surface just before it becomes leather hard will leave an interesting grid design in the ware. This surface texture will aid the glaze as it tends to show highlights, because of the uneven surfacing.

A length of cotton cloth cut to resemble ribbon, then tied into a neat bow, will serve as the base for a ceramic pin. Dip the cotton ribbon bow into slip. As it begins to set, shape it carefully. If in doubt as to the amount of slip absorbed by the cotton, paint the entire bow again with a brush first dipped into water and then into slip. When this is fired, the clay ribbon bow will be bisqued, the cotton will burn out. ●

Earring backs and pins are called "findings" and may be ready-bought from suppliers.

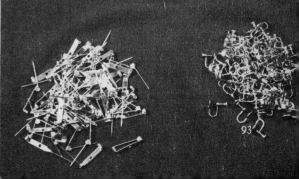

Build a Potter's Wheel

Whether foot-powered or electric, your pottery

efforts will revolve around an efficient wheel.

IT HAS been said that our civilization revolves on "the wheel." In a larger sense this is true, since without the wheel as a basic part of all machinery, whether ground to an eccentric or cut into a cog, basically it still is a wheel. In pottery, too, the wheel has always been of extreme importance.

The reference wheel refers to a circular disc, free to revolve on an axis placed exactly at the center of the disc and at right angles to the disc. The shaft upon which the disc revolves should be absolutely vertical. It should be supported by smooth-running bearings or sleeves.

There are many uses to which a wheel may be put. It is customary to employ a wheel for the purpose for which the particular wheel is designed. The simplest type of wheel is a whirler, or banding wheel. This wheel is used for designing or sketching a design in regular thickness completely around your ware. The gold band around the edge of a plate or the stripe of color around the base or mid-section of a lamp or cup are just a few of the uses of a banding wheel. An incised design may be cut with extreme regularity into your piece by the use of a banding wheel or whirler.

In building a piece of ware by the coil method, a whirler will save walking around the piece. In glazing, too, a revolving table or whirler is useful since all sides may be glazed or decorated without moving from your original position. All sides are equally exposed by revolving your wheel.

In sculpting it is necessary to view your piece and work your ware from all sides. A whirler eliminates the necessity of moving around the piece to work. It also permits building an arm or hand rest on one side next to the wheel and working on all sides without shifting your arm rest.

An inexpensive potter's wheel or whirler can be made from a wire-spool, pipe and fittings.

An ordinary nipple used by the plumbing profession is put in the spool to serve as an axle.

Locknuts are used to tighten the ends of the nipple. Make one end flush to plaster bat.

As at left, axle is extended to desired height, then is placed in shaft for free rotation.

A sleeve, or bushing, of approximately the same diameter as shaft serves as bearing.

How to Make a Whirler

A simple whirler can be made from a spool. Obtain a spool with flanges not less than 6″ in diameter. The spool should be wood or metal. Metal is preferable. Such a spool is usually used for winding or dispensing wire or ribbon. This spool will have a hole through the axle. Place a short piece of pipe (threaded on both ends) through this axle. Secure a bushing on top of the spool, tightening it on the pipe. Secure a coupling on the bottom of the pipe to draw up tight to the bottom of the spool. Affix into the other end of the coupling a two-foot piece of pipe. Insert this two-foot pipe into another piece of pipe just large enough to allow the spool and the two-foot piece of pipe to revolve freely. Use strap iron to secure the outer pipe in a vertical position at a convenient height. Upon the top of the spool drill three holes at irregular positions. Drive a Parker screw point up through each of these holes. Take a plaster bat, drill a hole part way through from the bottom for the bushing on top of the spool, and drill three small holes for the Parker screw points to fit snugly. This procedure will hold the plaster bat level on the spool and will keep it from shifting.

In constructing a kick wheel, the first step is to build a sturdy table to support wheel arrangement.

The legs of the table are braced all around to give it maximum stability. Bolts are unnecessary.

Below, the top of the table is made to fit type of wheel you plan to use. Note reinforcing at the top.

With wheel and pulley all set up, kick wheel is set for operation. Foot pedal should be hinged to floor.

How to Construct a Kick Wheel

To construct a kick wheel, it is necessary to understand that the power is supplied by foot. Hence, for convenience and comfort it should be built with a seat for the operator. His feet may dangle comfortably so that one foot may kick out to revolve a larger floor wheel. The construction is not involved. Erect a narrow table 36" high, 12" wide, and 30" long, well braced and cross-braced to insure rigidity. Obtain an old grinding wheel or similar wheel which is heavy. This wheel should be between 22" and 26" in diameter. Obtain a small wheel for the head or working wheel; this wheel should be between 8" and 12"

in diameter. The working (head) wheel will have to be flanged on the underside to permit the securing of an axle. This axle will then penetrate through the center of the table 4" from the side on which the operator will be seated. The axle will extend through the table and through the large heavy wheel. It will continue to the floor, where there should be a flange to keep the axle from end thrust or shifting. The female portion of the flange may receive a marble or steel ball upon which the solid axle may float. The large heavy wheel should be secured rigidly to the axle so that a kicking action on this wheel will revolve the axle and operate the working top.

Underside of the wheel shows the reduction pulley and speed control system. A motor may be attached.

The Power Wheel

The foregoing may be used as basic designs for a power wheel. Add a pulley to the shaft and set up an electric motor with a pulley. A belt between these pulleys will provide power drive. The smaller the driving pulley and the larger the driven pulley, the slower the speed. Most power wheels, however, are equipped with variable speed devices. Variable speed may be achieved by several methods. Arrange your motor with a loose belt and add in the path of the belt another pulley on a free axle. The axle bearing should be secured in slots so that pressure exerted by the foot pedal shifts the axle to increase tension on the belt, or by releasing pressure on this axle, belt slippage permits slower operation. Another arrangement of speed control is achieved by movable shivs on a split pulley. This automatically varies speed by changing the ratio of the pulleys. Another wheel manufacturer employs a sewing machine type motor where a foot-controlled rheostat diminishes power and hence speed, at will. Still another design employs a geared motor for speed control. •

How to Figure Motor Size

To determine the size of electric motor needed for a given job, the formula may be used:

$$\frac{\text{HP Output Reqd.}}{\text{ME} \times \text{PF} \times \text{LE}} = \text{size of motor needed}$$

Where:
HP Output Reqd. is the power required to move the loaded machine
ME is the motor efficiency.
PF equals power factor.
LE is line efficiency, or voltage output divided by voltage input.

For example: An electric motor is required to operate a shale planer which when under load puts a demand of 50 horsepower on the power source. Power at the plant's connection to a nearby public power line is 440 volts, but due to the resistance of the No. 2 wire used to span the 2,000 ft. distance to the shale planer, the power at the motor is only 410 volts. With a motor of 85 per cent efficiency, in a plant where the power factor is 85 per cent, the formula becomes:

$$\frac{50}{.85 \times .85 \times \dfrac{410}{440}} = \text{size of motor needed}$$

$$\frac{50}{.723 \times .93} = \text{size of motor needed}$$

$$\frac{50}{} = 74.6 \text{ or a 75 HP motor is needed}$$

volts. With a motor of 85 percent efficiency,

Using the Potter's Wheel

Master the art of throwing and raising shapes on this versatile clayworking tool.

Y OUR wheel will be helpful in doing pottery. The use of a simple whirler is a means of banding, striping, or incising. It is an aid if not a necessity in sculpting. Glazing, even fettling and trimming, can be made easier by the use of a wheel. Your kick or power wheel is a necessity in throwing and raising a shape. This same wheel will enable you to make, trim, and decorate the most intricate of pieces.

To set up your whirler or banding wheel for decorating or striping, sit or stand, as you prefer, for comfort. The wheel should be in front of you, slightly left or right, depending upon which hand you use for

work. Rest the forearm from elbow to wrist on a solid platform, either made for that purpose or by stacking books for a rest, or by obtaining a box whose side will serve as an arm rest. Grasp the tool or brush firmly, as you would a pencil, using the index, middle finger, and thumb. Pivot or control spacing with the pinkie. Allow free wrist action. Use the other hand to revolve the wheel. Your piece should be mounted upon a plaster bat. You should make or have bats of various sizes. Each bat you use should be centered on its wheel head. Bought wheels usually have concentric circles scored into the surface to aid in centering. In the event you are using a homemade wheel, you will find that by rotating the wheel rapidly with one hand and using the fingers of the other hand, lightly touching the plaster bat, you will feel the thrust of uneven centering. Slight pressure of the fingers touching the bat will center the bat. Once this is done, secure the bat by the method described in the previous chapter. You should have several bats so fitted in different sizes. This enables you to remove the bat from the wheel without touching the piece on which you are working until it has attained leather hardness.

Pottery Repairs

Sometimes a piece of pottery will not adhere well where joined in the bisque fire. Fit the separated parts together well and make sure that they do fit. If such is the case, these pieces may be coated with sodium silicate at the break and pressed together. There are regular commercial bisque cements which may be used in the same way. If, however, the ware is broken and the break is not clean, adhere as much of the ware at the break as you can. Make a paste by using the same type of clay as you do for your ware. This clay flour must be calcined (fired in its dry powdery state). Mixed calcined clay with sodium silicate and fill the area of the break. Now your piece is ready to glaze and fire.

In the event the broken piece is glazed when it breaks, it may be treated the same way and reglazed. Be sure that you use only calcined clay, as plastic or raw clay will shrink unevenly and part from bisque ware.

A great variety of designs and shapes can be made on the modern potter's wheel, as illustrated below.

Below, lumps of soft clay are used to fasten the plaster bat to wheel head in pottery preparation.

The potter's wheel is also used in decorating work. Important: control speed and keep your wrist free.

The Modern Potter's Wheel and its Accessories

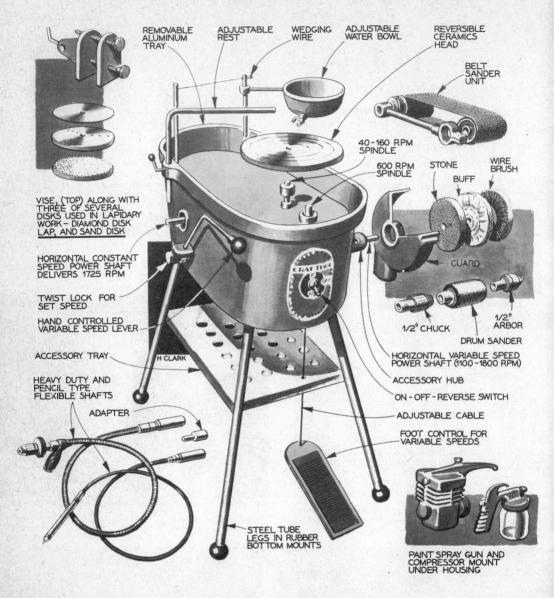

REMOVABLE ALUMINUM TRAY

ADJUSTABLE REST

WEDGING WIRE

ADJUSTABLE WATER BOWL

REVERSIBLE CERAMICS HEAD

BELT SANDER UNIT

40-160 RPM SPINDLE

600 RPM SPINDLE

STONE

BUFF

WIRE BRUSH

GUARD

VISE, (TOP) ALONG WITH THREE OF SEVERAL DISKS USED IN LAPIDARY WORK – DIAMOND DISK LAP, AND SAND DISK

HORIZONTAL CONSTANT SPEED POWER SHAFT DELIVERS 1725 RPM

TWIST LOCK FOR SET SPEED

HAND CONTROLLED VARIABLE SPEED LEVER

ACCESSORY TRAY

H CLARK

1/2" CHUCK

1/2" ARBOR

DRUM SANDER

HORIZONTAL VARIABLE SPEED POWER SHAFT (1100-1800 RPM)

ACCESSORY HUB

ON - OFF - REVERSE SWITCH

ADJUSTABLE CABLE

FOOT CONTROL FOR VARIABLE SPEEDS

HEAVY DUTY AND PENCIL TYPE FLEXIBLE SHAFTS

ADAPTER

STEEL TUBE LEGS IN RUBBER BOTTOM MOUNTS

PAINT SPRAY GUN AND COMPRESSOR MOUNT UNDER HOUSING

CRAFTOOL

Pottery Points

All movable parts of your equipment, such as motors, shafts, bearings, etc., should be lubricated at regular intervals.

Avoid contact with electric switches while the hands are moist. Most potter's wheels have a foot switch.

Always clean up after using pottery equipment. It will save hours of labor later if you clean up while your material is still plastic.

Do not be discouraged. All potter's shelves are lined with second

The Craftool is a representative type of potter's wheel. Top can easily be lifted out for cleaning.

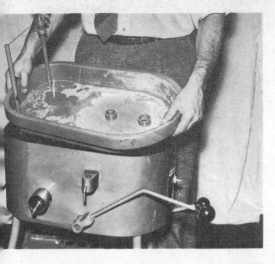

A flat sanding wheel is an extremely useful tool that can be used directly attached to the whirler.

An arbor is also available to the potter and can be equipped with a chuck for horizontal drilling.

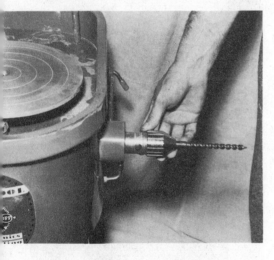

The arbor can also be used for grinding with an abrasive wheel and a guard attached, as shown.

With an idler attachment the arbor accepts standard abrasive belt for sanding and rubbing of ware.

Wire brushes or drum sanders (shown below) are yet another use of horizontal accessory hubshaft.

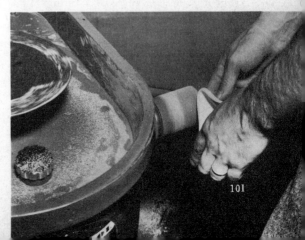

A pot of specific dimensions should be made with just so much clay. Here clay is weighed out before throwing.

Three Lions

Throwing on a Potter's Wheel

The first rule of successful throwing upon the kick or power wheel is to make sure your clay is thoroughly wedged. When you are sure of the proper condition of your clay, start by placing a round piece of clay on the plaster bat mounted on your wheel. The bat should be clean and moist. Keep a container of water handy, since the clay must be kept wet while turning. In placing clay on the bat, slap your clay down fairly hard, as near center as possible. Start your wheel fairly rapidly. Put both hands upon the clay while the wheel is revolving. You will feel the unevenness by the clay's thumping against your fingers. The object in centering is to eliminate this vibration, so that as the wheel and clay revolve there is no noticeable thump. You must control the clay while the wheel is turning. Exert the necessary strength to dominate. If necessary, brace your arms on rests—do not bend your wrists. Keep the arms braced against the sides of the body. Keep the clay wet by splashing water on the piece while working. The proper amount of moisture is something you can learn only by experience. Too much moisture will allow the piece to collapse; too little water will make it impossible to center. The hands must never be dry. Your head should be held looking down on your

The basic step in successful pottery throwing is to make certain that the clay is thoroughly wedged. The wheel is equipped with a taut wire which is used for this purpose. The Craftool also has a basin for water, as clay must be kept moist while it is turned.

102

work. The clay should never be allowed to feel sticky while working at the wheel.

There are two distinct operations with the wheel. The first of these is throwing. This consists of centering and then, by manipulation with the fingers and by pressure upon the clay, raising or shaping the piece. As soon as the piece is raised or hollowed by hand, wipe off excess moisture. Remove the bat and allow the ware to stand until it can support itself. As the piece begins to dry, it will separate from the bat easily. Now place the leather hard ware upon a clean bat.

To center the piece, hold the fingers loosely around the piece as the wheel revolves slowly, and shift the ware until it revolves without touching the fingers or hand at any point. When you have located your piece, place several wads of clay against the ware and on the revolving head. This will keep the ware from being hurled off the table by centrifugal force. Now you may use your turning tools to design or to turn the bottom, or to incise the outer surface. Be sure you do not gouge too deeply or score too deeply. The fingers will do very well in turning down a lip or flare.

You may, if you wish, leave the marks that denote wheel work to identify the piece, or these may be fettled off by using a moist sponge while rotating the disc.

Such items as teapots and cups are fashioned by wheel. Spouts and handles are added after the piece is turned. These are shaped by the coil method and adhered by the use of slip.

On this and on the following two pages are shown in step-by-step photographs the approved techniques used by expert potters in throwing a tall bowl, or curved pitcher, on the potter's wheel. Study this series before you actually try throwing. •

With the clay properly wetted and the plaster bat in place, throw clay onto wheel's center.

Form the clay into a mound by gentle pressure of the hands. Try to maintain an even speed.

With one hand, lower the mound of clay to a workable base. Support by other hand.

Open the clay with the thumbs and your piece will start to take shape. Keep the clay wet.

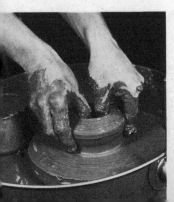

Control the contour with sure hands and support outside walls or clay will be shapeless.

With piece beginning to shape up, slow wheel down and check for flaws. Also trim off.

103

How to Throw a Curved Pitcher

After the cone is raised in the clay mound and then lowered, begin to shape the walls of the pitcher.

When the hollow has been developed evenly, begin to shape the cylinder, starting with flare at top.

Raise the cylinder of the pitcher to its required height, then commence to shape the rounded body.

In starting the flare, proper procedure is to give support to inside wall while pressing with fingers.

Now concave curve is made at the bottom of pitcher by pressing a finger to the base, held against hand.

Your next step is to thin out the top and widen the flare by holding a wire tool lightly against shape.

Since the pitcher is rather deep, a sponge on the end of a dowel is good for smoothing inside walls.

At this point, widen the rounded body of the piece with a wood or cardboard scraper held at angle.

To trim the base, apply a knife or strip of metal to the base, holding it at the angle you require.

To complete the trimming of the base, strip away excess clay by hand, rolling it into small balls.

The pouring spout is made with the wheel stationary. Note that one hand guides, the other braces.

The final step is attaching the handle. Technique is to roll it to size and impress by coil method.

These pitchers, mass-produced for marketing, are only one of many items a ceramic hobbyist can sell.

You Can Make
Your Hobby Pay

**There's a waiting market for your ware if you can fill a need.
The pay from clay will support your studio—and show a profit.**

THE chapters previous to this have touched upon methods and applications. They have been meant as a guide and as answers to the many questions which will occur as you work with clay. After the first rush of enthusiasm in doing all kinds of projects you have dreamed of, you will slow down and cast about for new and unusual ideas, particularly those which will enable you to market your ware, thus making your hobby self-supporting; in fact, earning enough to equip your clay shop with much more equipment and still show a profit. No matter what your ability, there are always items to be made which will find a ready market.

For the clay hobbyist who enjoys such pottery as limited artistic ability will permit, there are always molds. These need not be original. The Madonna head mold and molds of the figures of The Nativity will make an excellent project. These pieces, cast in white slip and glazed with only clear glaze, will make ideal settings for flower arrangements which will be absorbed by any florist shop selling flower arrangements and table decorations. A holly leaf, curled and rolled back to allow for drilling a hole to permit use of this ornament as a candleholder is an item of extreme seasonal popularity. This is glazed green, and includes a small cluster of clay berries placed around the hole. The berries are colored red with nail polish after the finished piece comes from the kiln.

Plates have a source of financial stability which has supported many potteries. These, too, are made by mold or by wheel. All types of shapes can be formed by either mold or wheel. The regular shape derived from this method can easily be altered by pinching or flattening parts that are rounded. This must be done, of course, while the clay is very soft.

Efficient kiln operation can provide a full quota of income-producing table ware and molded figures.

For the clay hobbyist who has ability to shape attractive pieces by hand, such items as unusual lamps—shaped like a ming tree, or made of slabs embossed with various types of leaves (some leaves flattened onto the surface and others curled away slightly) will prove remunerative.

Ceramic kitchen equipment, such as a gravy spoon drip, spice boxes, salt and pepper shakers, always find a ready market. Pipe racks, ashtrays, the big roomy kind, cigarette boxes, flowerholders (frogs) will find a demand at art and giftware shops. Personalized items bearing initials or embossing indicating meaning to the purchaser create a demand which frequently results in snowballing sales. A half pitcher, backed by a slab, makes an attractive wall hanging. To make this, pour a small pitcher or vase. Cut it vertically in half. Back the cut portion with a smooth slab of clay and seal the junction with slip. This operation is then applied to the remaining half, and thus two wall ornaments are created.

Gaily colored Christmas tree ornaments will be popular now since former sources of this material are not as readily available as previously. Many items can be combined, as, a cigarette box lid may have a mold of a dog secured as a handle. An ashtray may often be decorated with flowers or figurines.

Piggy banks, salad bowls and plates, mixing bowls, flower planters, jewelry, buttons, and canisters are always in demand. Ceramic tumblers keep most liquids cooler than most types of vessels, and are popular.

An hors d'oeuvres platter made of wood in circular shape will support ceramic sections shaped like pie cuts. Construct or buy a circular tray 15"-18" in diameter. Lightly mark a 4" circle in the center. From the outside circumference of this circle mark spokes to the circumference of the tray which will divide your tray into six equal pie-shaped sections. This type of serving tray is a popular seller at all gift shops.

Look around your home and realize how many items made of wood, metal, or plaster can be duplicated or improved upon by use of ceramics. Doll's heads and doll parts (arms, legs, etc.) are needed by doll manufacturers as well as doll hospitals. One hobbyist specializes in making miniature doll plates with miniature food portions upon them. These pieces are first shaped and decorated with the colors to resemble the food (such as a piece of steak, or an ear of corn, or a heap of peas and potatoes, all on a miniature plate). Fruit shapes, used for ice cube caddies, jelly jars, olive dishes,

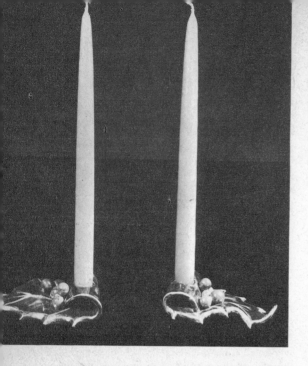

Candlesticks of a seasonal design glazed in bright colors will prove a ready seller at Christmas time.

celery and pickle servers, are attractive gifts which can be made cheaply by the ceramist. Icebox or refrigerator trays or bowls with close-fitting lids, gaily colored, are also items which will find no resistance from the gift seeker. There is no limit to the number of popular and interesting things you can do to earn extra money. By applying the basic methods explained in this book, nothing is beyond your imagination in ceramics. There are many industrial necessities, such as special insulators for hard to reach locations where only special shapes can be used.

Your source of sales will depend upon the area in which you reside. If in a rural district, your own display, set up for passing motorists to admire, will be one way of showing and selling your ware. Place little cards on your stand advising purchasers that you will ship small souvenir pins as requested, and will also fill Christmas and birthday orders by mail. Occasional trips showing your ware to church groups and your novelty store at your shopping center will arouse considerable interest.

If you live in a suburban area, there will be many decorator's shops, florists, gift shops, and stationery stores for you to consider as prospects. These folks will not only express interest in what you are doing but will give you many ideas, too.

If you reside in a large city, check your

large specialty shops and florists to see what items are most popular and in demand. Check the prices, allow between 40% and 50% for the retailer, and you'll discover the approximate cost. This will allow you to figure competitive prices and determine about what price you can obtain from the dealer. There are also novelty jobbers who can use the full output of many ceramic studios. However, here the selling price must be low, since the jobber gets paid a percentage ranging from 10% to 25%, and the retailer must mark up the ware between 40% and 50%.

Several fine ceramists make display cabinets and fill them with samples of their products. They lend these display cases and samples to various gift shops, with the understanding that the cabinets and ware belong to the ceramist. The proceeds of any merchandise which is sold are turned over to the ceramist, less an agreed percentage which is retained by the store. This type of sale is known as doing business on consignment. It is helpful to both the partners, since the store acquires no liability and yet has both merchandise and display case to enhance sales, and the ceramist, because of this inducement to the retailer, is enabled to find many outlets in which no sales resistance is encountered.

Many of the national periodicals feature a section in which novelties are sold by mail order. Mail order advertising is expensive but usually brings satisfactory results. This would be so with many small items, such as a miniature ceramic well-and-bucket, set up to serve as a postal scale and stamp dispenser. Many such ideas have already been patented, and it would be well before embarking on a venture of this type to check first the infringement possibilities. You might also check the postal regulations through your local postmaster.

Ideas which will prove ceramics a useful hobby are a result of employing your skill in the creation of both beautiful and interesting, useful ware. Important questions to ask are these: Has it eye appeal? Has it utility? If you can answer "yes" to either of these, your piece will be a success. By employing the information imparted in this book, you can make many items for your home, which will in themselves not only prove helpful but will also have value as samples which will stimulate your guests and friends to ask for replicas. Many such items have been dealt with in the previous chapters and would not bear repetition; however, other items are herein enumerated.

Ceramic mail boxes will withstand

These figurines are ready for glazing in brilliant colors and will form creches, or Nativity groups.

change in temperature and variable weather. Ceramic handles on light fixtures, toilet chains, Venetian blinds, and window stays will be far easier to keep clean than wood, papier mache, or other materials. Fireplace mantels or ornaments can be designed and decorated by indicating personalized influence, such as initials, favorite sayings, or baby's birthday or weight. Personal cups with initials incised or embossed for each member of the family, napkin rings of a general family pattern, each in a different color, ceramic racks for carving knife or fork or for gravy spoons—these are practically a must in today's household.

Ceramic containers in which will fit your can of scouring powder for bathroom use is an ideal camouflage for unsightly cans. Ceramic soap dish and toothbrush holders are extremely useful, even though mortality is high. Many pieces of household impedimenta are readily available in the open market, but frequently it is impossible to obtain such ware in desirable colors. This obstacle you are now able to overcome, since any and all colors are available to you.

Checkers, chess men, washrag hooks, fancy shoe buckles, tie clips, lamps and finials, powder boxes, jewelry receptacles, pin trays, perfume burners, brush and comb receptacles—all will prove useful besides affording tremendous satisfaction in the realization that this ware is personalized. Tumblers, serving bowls, coasters, almond dishes, candy boxes, window decorations, planters of all types—will provide useful and colorful ceramic pieces.

In hospital work ceramics are employed as a valuable field in occupational therapy. Here the patient learns the necessary manipulation required in handling plastics. He learns that in spite of his handicap, no matter what it may be, he can shape a piece to his desires and give it an aura of permanence. He will learn patience and will find a stimulation which will need no prodding. With these folks it is necessary to resort to simple beginnings, preferably the coil or slab method, and to encourage each step of progress they display. Criticism, if any, must be wholly constructive. Nothing will restore confidence for such a patient so much as the realization that he, too, can construct or form ware solely.

through his own ability, and bring a formless lump of clay into a thing of beauty and utility.

There are many projects dealt with herein for both the resident patient and the out patient which will find hospital use—such as ice-cream dishes, tumblers, flower vases, water pitchers, and many other types of ceramic dispensers so necessary in hospitals. There are many items which these people can make having market value and which can be sold in order to help make the patient financially independent, as well as provide a means for the institution to recover part of its costs, at least, in marketing such ware. Florist shops which deliver their ware to such institutions are an ideal source or an outlet. Nurses, internes, and nurse's aides make an ideal promotional force in advertising such ware by word of mouth.

There are limitless uses for ceramics in the garden, such as ceramic rings to support peonies to stakes, clay flower pots, large ceramic bowls in which to plant tender plants like fig trees so that during the winter months the whole bowl may be lifted without disturbing the plant's roots, small ceramic grills for borders in a garden are frequently made of red clay and are unglazed.

Garden ornaments now frequently made of cement may be fashioned by hand or by the mold method. These pieces may be glazed to appear more lifelike and will withstand the rigors of all types of weather. Ceramic trellises for such delicate plants as sweet peas will enhance the beauty of the flower. An outdoor garden pool, lined with ceramic tile, will probably remain watertight far longer than any other type of construction. Oriental gardens around such a pool showing figures of men and women, rustic bridges, tea houses, pagodas, will resemble the real thing when made from clay.

Lawn markers with the resident's name or initials, plant identifiers, and labels in trees will all retain their fresh newness of appearance during the passage of years. Ceramic table tops for garden furniture will withstand acid tests as well as the weather.

Ceramics as an industrial item find only specialized application. There are such firms as Centralab Division of Globe Union, Inc. of Milwaukee, who use ceramics because of their superiority as dielectric capacitors. Magnetic Spinels, in Butler, New Jersey, who are engaged in manufacturing ceramic yokes for television tubes, also use ceramics in great quantities. Many of the industrial ceramics in the Midwest are turning to steatites primarily because of their higher insulation resistance. It is these factors which are rapidly increasing the demand for ceramic products commercially and in industry.

Hartford Fans Co., in Hartford, Connecticut, which plant has, according to Bud Rankin, expanded "from mixing slip in a bucket to a blunger which is large enough to swim in," is still expanding.

Many of our household appliances are made of ceramic ware. Gas range handles, faucet handles, toilet bowls, basins, sinks, and bathtubs are all fashioned from the lowly mud we call clay. They go through the same process of vitrification and glazing. Porcelain sockets, automobile spark plug holders, fine hospital filters, power line and telephone company insulators are all forms of ceramics. The ceramics industry is truly a field upon whose shoulders rests the financial stability of many people all over the world.

A wide range of ceramic subjects readily lend themselves to the coil method, which requires no special equipment. Here are three animals and a vase made in this way.

Glossary of Ceramic Terms

APPENDAGE—An added part, i.e., a handle or spout.

ARABIC—Gum used as a binder for clay or glaze.

ARMATURE—Skeleton frame or support upon which to build ware.

BALL MILL—A jar or container holding balls or pebbles which cause grinding when the container is rotated.

BAT—Slab made of plaster, usually with a flat surface.

BISQUE OR BISCUIT—Clay which has been hardened by exposure to high temperature.

BLOCK—A master mold made from the model. From this, case molds are formed.

BLOWING—Bursting of ware.

BLUNGER—A container with an agitator for mixing material.

BODY STAINS—Coloring agents used to modify color or shade of clay.

BODY—The essential part, as in clay or glaze.

BONE DRY—Thoroughly air-dried ready to fire.

BOXWOOD TOOLS—Wood instruments for working and designing in clay.

CALCINE—To heat-treat.

CASE—A copy or reproduction from the block.

CARBONATES—Chemicals used for achieving color in glaze.

CAST—To make by pouring, as in molds.

CERAMICS—An art covering industrial, commercial, and fine art work, using clay bodies.

CHINA—Porcelain so called because it originally came from China.

CHINA CLAY—(Kaolin) Weather-aged rock of the igneous type.

CLAY—Alumina and Silica in soft condition from which pottery is made.

CLAY FLOUR—Refined powdered clay not calcined; usually 200 mesh or finer.

COIL—An extruded piece of clay usually made by rolling a worm-shaped piece of clay by hand.

CONE—Mixture of clay and glaze with a predetermined melting point.

CRACKLE—Deliberate fine hairline cracks in glazed body developed during and after fire.

CRAWL—Term applied to glaze which gathers in lumps rather than flows out during fire.

CRAZE—Same as crackle, but not by design.

DEFLOCCULANT—Silicate and Soda—water wetter.

ELECTROLYTES—(See deflocculant).

ELEPHANT EAR—A type of fine, thin sponge used for fettling; similar to a facial sponge.

EMBOSSING—A type of decoration in which a design is raised upon the surface of the ware.

ELEMENT—Coiled resistance wire for heating the kiln electrically.

ENGOBE—Colored clay used for design work.

FAIENCE—Decorated earthenware as distinct from tableware; a method of covering one color clay with another color clay.

FELDSPAR—Fusible type of stone used in preparing certain clays.

FETTLE—To remove imperfections from ware.

FETTLING KNIFE—A sharp, flexible-bladed knife similar to a paring knife.

FIRE—To heat or expose ware to high temperatures.

FLINT—A form of stone, mostly silica, added to clay bodies or to glazes.

FRIT—Ingredients similar to glass components, water suspendable.

FURNITURE—Refers to kiln or oven ware—shelves, stilts, posts, etc.

GLAZE—A glassy material in pulverized state.

GLOSS—Shiny.

GLOST—As applied to glaze firing.

GREEN—Unfired ware.

GROG—Ground bisque ware.

GUM—See Arabic, tragacanth.

INCISING—Cutting, as in a design.

JEWELRY CEMENT—Used in adhering metal backings to ceramics, for earrings, etc.

KAOLIN—See China clay.

KILN—Heat treating oven.

KILN-GARD—A limiting device for turning off kiln automatically; cone-activated.

KILN WASH—Material used as protective covering to absorb glaze drips; usually ½ Kaolin and ½ flint.

LEATHER, OR LEATHER HARD—Clay partially dried.

MAJOLICA—Colored opaque glaze.

MATT—A finish with only semi-gloss texture, i.e., egg shell.

MENDING SLIP—Water and clay mixed to the consistency of light cream to adhere two unfired clay surfaces.

MOLD—Hollow shape into which plastic material is pressed or poured.

MUFFLE—Inner lining of heating chamber of kiln.

OVERGLAZE—Decoration applied after glaze fire.

OXIDES—Used as agents to induce color during firing.

PEELING—A defect between clay and glaze.

PLASTIC—Soft, able to be shaped.

POLYCHROME—A form of decoration where one color engobe is scratched and the route so made is filled with another color engobe.

POTTERY—The art of making earthenware.

POTTER'S PLASTER—A lightweight plaster, quick-setting, basically pulverized gypsum.

POURING—Filling a mold with liquid clay.

PROJECT—A plan or course of action.

PRESS MOLD—A shape into which plastic clay is forced, then partly dried and removed.

PROPS—Kiln shelf supports.

PYROMETER—A temperature indicator.

REDUCTION—Applies to firing method burning a material during firing to reduce the oxygen in the kiln for the effect on glazes.

REFRACTORY—Refers to heat-resistant material.

ROUTILE—Chemical causing antique finish.

SEPARATOR—A coating applied to permit separation of mold and model.

SGRAFFITO—Scratching in a design.

SHIVERING—Poor adherence between glaze and body.

SLIP—Liquid clay.

SLIP DECORATION—See engobe.

SLIP TRACER—A syringe from which slip is forced to trace a raised design.

SPURS—Small webbed stilts.

SCRAPER—Watchmakers' steel sheets shaped for use in fettling or forming objects.

SPATULA—Used as scraper, same as kitchen spatula.

STILTS—Small rests made of refractory material to separate ware from shelf or floor of kiln during glost fire.

TEMPLATE—An outline for form, used as a guide.

THERMOCOUPLE—Two dissimilar metals welded at the tip, which when heated generate microvoltage to operate the pyrometer.

THROWING—Forming a piece by the potter's wheel.

TILES—Usually refer to either manufactured or self-made shapes, oblong, round, square, elliptical—used for decorative pieces.

TRAGACANTH—A gum used to aid in adhering glaze to bisque, also a binder.

TURNING—The art of completing a leathery piece of ware by rotating upon a wheel and using tools.

UNDERGLAZE—Pottery colors used for decoration—these colors are flat.

VITRIFY—Fire to stone hardness.

WATER SMOKE—Chemical moisture leaving the ware during bisque fire.

WEDGING—The preparation of clay by removing air bubbles.

WEDGING BOARD—Plaster-covered area with wire cutter used for wedging clay.

WHIRLER—A revolving stand or table, usually rotated by hand.

WHEEL—A potter's wheel driven by hand, foot, or electric power.

WIRE AND TOOLS—Usually wood stock, though some are metal stock with various wire shaped ends for work in clay modeling.